Building a Robust Work Environment to Help Drive Your Total Rewards Strategy

culture
at work

G. Michael Barton, SPHR
Author of *Recognition at Work*

About WorldatWork®

WorldatWork (www.worldatwork.org) is the association for human resources professionals focused on attracting, motivating and retaining employees. Founded in 1955, WorldatWork provides practitioners with knowledge leadership to effectively implement total rewards — compensation, benefits, work-life, performance and recognition, development and career opportunities — by connecting employee engagement to business performance. WorldatWork supports its 30,000 members and customers in 30 countries with thought leadership, education, publications, research and certification.

The WorldatWork group of registered marks includes: WorldatWork®, workspan®, Certified Compensation Professional or CCP®, Certified Benefits Professional® or CBP, Global Remuneration Professional or GRP®, Work-Life Certified Professional or WLCP™, WorldatWork Society of Certified Professionals®, and Alliance for Work-Life Progress® or AWLP®.

Any laws, regulations or other legal requirements noted in this publication are, to the best of the publisher's knowledge, accurate and current as of this book's publishing date. WorldatWork is providing this information with the understanding that WorldatWork is not engaged, directly or by implication, in rendering legal, accounting or other related professional services. You are urged to consult with an attorney, accountant or other qualified professional concerning your own specific situation and any questions that you may have related to that.

This book is published by WorldatWork. The interpretations, conclusions and recommendations in this book are those of the author and do not necessarily represent those of WorldatWork.

© 2006 WorldatWork
ISBN 1-57963-1584 (Paperback/softback)
    978-157963-234-2 (E-book)

No portion of this publication may be reproduced in any form without express written permission from WorldatWork.

www.worldatwork.org

Acknowledgments

WorldatWork Press would like to thank the following technical reviewers for helping to shape and strengthen the content of this book:

M. Michael Markowich, DPA, President, Markowich Consulting Group

Linda McKee, CCP, Human Resource Manager, Honeywell

Rodger D. Stotz, CCP, Vice President, Managing Consultant Maritz Inc.

WorldatWork Staff Contributors
Wendy Anderson, Editorial Assistant

Daniel Cafaro, Book Publishing Manager

Rebecca Williams Ficker, Production Manager

Christina Fuoco, Editor

Alan Luu, Graphic Designer

Rose Stanley, Practice Leader

Table of Contents

Introduction: Why Is Culture So Important? 1
Are Values and Culture One in the Same? 4
Objectives 5
Cultural Drivers 5

Chapter 1: Defining Culture 7
Importance of Culture 16
Matching Culture with Strategic Goals 18
Impact of Culture on Total Rewards Programs 20

Chapter 2: Cultural Diversity 27
Diversity Factors 33
Integrating Diversity with Culture 33
Assessing the Organization's Commitment 39
Designing a Diversity Training Program 39
Aligning Total Rewards with Diversity 43

Chapter 3: Developing Cultural Goals 47
Designing a Cultural Profile 50
Measuring the Effectiveness of the Culture 54
Aligning Organizational Strategy with Cultural Goals 58

Chapter 4: Environment Versus Culture 61
Defining Environment 61
Comparing Culture and Environment 65
Linking Culture with Environment 67
Developing Environment-Friendly Total Rewards Programs 71
Branding Environment Programs 73

Chapter 5: Dealing with Value Conflicts 77
Identifying Value Conflicts 79
Creating a Value Culture 81
Ensuring "Organizational Fit" 83
Integrating Values with Total Rewards 85

Chapter 6: Developing a Cultural Chain 89
The Customer Value Chain 91
Defining Customer Value 93
Matching Culture with Customer Service Goals 95

Chapter 7: Ongoing Cultural Development 97
Cultural Surveys 99
Policy Audits 100
Readiness Assessment 102
Soliciting and Maintaining Management Support .103
Ongoing Communication 105

Chapter 8: Case Study 109
Wegmans Food Markets 111

Appendices 115
Workplace Diversity Strategy 117
Sample Code of Conduct 120
Sample Policy and Procedure 122
Sample Cultural Survey 126
Policy Audit 128
Sample Talking Points for Cultural Diversity Program 130
Sample Communication Plan 132
Flexible Work Schedules Survey 134
Web Site Resources 154

Introduction

Why Is Culture So Important?

Creating the right culture for employees is a major challenge for organizations and their leaders. However, the reward for developing a culture that employees and other key stakeholders can embrace pays big dividends for the organization. These dividends include lower job vacancy rates, reduced employee turnover, higher employee morale, enhanced public image and increased customer loyalty. The "100 Best Companies To Work For," published annually by *Fortune* magazine, would certainly support building a strong culture. Figure 1 summarizes some of the approaches that the "100 Best Companies" have taken, using culture as its ally. One unique quote (*Fortune*, Jan. 24, 2005) referring to the top company in the "100 Best" may sum up how culture impacts the employee:

"The Wegmans' culture is bigger than Danny (Wegman) in the same way that Wal-Mart's became bigger than Sam (Walton)."

FIGURE 1 Summary of the Cultural Approaches by Five of the '100 Best Companies to Work For'

Company	Rank	Unique Cultural Approaches	Unique Rewards Programs
Wegmans Food Markets	1	• Company Motto: "Employees First, Second" Customers • Treat employees like family members • Passionate customer service • Loyal employees, low turnover • Empower employees to learn and handle problems	• Salaries are at the high end of the market • Gave $54 million for college scholarships • Generous training programs for employees
Cisco Systems	27	• Fun working environment	• "Nerd lunches" • Unique training opportunities
Four Seasons Hotels	51	• Make employees feel valued	• Employee of the year award selected by fellow employees
Vanguard Group	72	• Celebrate corporate anniversaries and achievements • Focus on employee and team achievements	• Vanguard Award for Excellence awarded by a select group of "crew members" • Vanguard Spot Bonus Award provided to crew members exhibiting exemplary services
Harley-Davidson	92	• 90% of the employees identify with the company's "riding culture"	• Employees get to work at biker rallies at Harley's expense

Although the leader certainly sets the tone, no one individual represents an organizational culture. For this reason, culture becomes the cornerstone of the work experience. Most individuals spend more time at work than they do with their families.

This is true even if some of that time is spent in front of a computer at home. The culture is still imbedded in the individual who works from home. Culture clearly defines how an employee feels about what they are doing and if it is worthwhile.

Rewards and incentives need to complement the culture if they are to be effective in motivating employees. Many organizations spend an enormous amount of money investing in incentive compensation or customized benefits plans that do little in the long run to motivate employees. The reason for this failure is the inability of the program to effectively tie in with and support the existing culture.

Culture, on the other hand, is the one component that does produce long-term benefits or can create major issues. How can this one component be so important? The obvious answer is the stable nature, for better or worse, of all cultures. The culture of an organization cannot be changed overnight because the people already there define it. Very few employees are willing or, for that matter, equipped, to make sudden and drastic changes in the way they think and believe. Culture is an integral part of the organization's belief system and as such forms the basis of the employment experience.

One of the biggest mistakes made by merging organizations is to believe culture will change in a short period of time. Some change experts predict that the merging of two cultures can take up to 10 years to be successful. Culture gives employees a positive or negative "comfort zone" that is difficult to overcome. Even in well-established cultures, change can be painstakingly difficult if key stakeholders see it as adversely impacting the culture.

Are Values and Culture One in the Same?

Organizations often have a wholesale list of values attached to their mission and vision statements. Values like:

- Teamwork
- Caring spirit
- Integrity
- Innovation
- Accountability
- Service excellence
- Personal fulfillment
- Trust.

However, the stated values may not necessarily represent the organization's "enacted" culture. Values can be statements of what leaders would like the organization to be.

The enacted or actual culture may be quite different than the values or mission statement. Values alone do not define the organization's culture. The intent of this publication is to explore how culture impacts how we work, reward, compensate and motivate employees. This book provides a framework for incorporating culture into the work experience. It explores all aspects of culture and its importance to employees and key stakeholders. It provides a comprehensive means for assessing and defining the organization's culture. This book also addresses how to incorporate culture in the organization's total rewards program. The book has seven objectives in reviewing this important workplace topic. Each objective builds on the other about how to manage and assess the organization's culture and environment.

Objectives

To define all the components of culture and how it fits with other total rewards programs.

- To develop strategies for integrating diversity into the organization's culture.
- To design and align organizational strategy with cultural goals and outcomes.
- To integrate the organization's culture with its environment.
- To identify and address value conflicts within the organization's culture.
- To align the organization's culture with the customer's value chain.
- To provide tools for conducting ongoing cultural reviews.

Cultural Drivers

Culture is central to the success of an organization and its members. It is a phenomenon that encompasses how we work, interact and organize our lives. If we work for an organization that has a strong and well-regarded culture, our approach to work-life is generally going to be positively impacted. There are number of drivers leading us to manage and assess this important work component. Figure 2 details some of the drivers for effectively managing culture.

The importance of each cultural driver will be discussed thoroughly in the following chapters of this publication. How each driver interacts to help the organization succeed and survive will be explored and fully developed. Culture is the one component often taken for granted in an organization's rewards program. Yet, culture provides leaders with a valuable tool to get employees and key stakeholders actively involved in the organization's success.

Culture is also a key component of WorldatWork's Total Rewards model. Culture is an integral part of the "work-life" component that focuses on the individual needs of the employee. As part of the work-life component, culture is an important initiative in creating support for work-life programs. Culture is also a determinant of how well unique programs, such as diversity education, women's advancement and mentoring, will be received. Organizational culture is also one of the three key drivers of the total rewards strategy. As a key driver, organizational culture impacts how new total rewards programs will be received and integrated into the organization. When crafting a total rewards strategy, it is imperative that organizational culture be addressed before deciding what total rewards programs to offer. Culture also has a major impact on all of the other elements of the total rewards model. It impacts how we design programs for compensation, benefits, performance and recognition, and development and career opportunities. Culture is a major resource for determining what the employees expect and what the organization is willing and able to provide in all of the total rewards elements. As we delve into this important topic, remember that culture establishes the expectations and norms of behavior that employees have formed and value. These expectations and norms of behavior ultimately impact the success or failure of the total rewards strategy.

Action and Discussion Points are sprinkled liberally throughout this publication. The purpose of these points is to provide helpful hints about how to effectively use the resources provided in the publication. The publication provides a template for assessing and managing an organizational culture. There is no "one-size-fits-all" approach to this subject. This publication will attempt to provide readers with tools that can be used and possibly adapted to their culture.

FIGURE 2 Cultural Drivers

Culture:
- Leadership
- Strategic planning
- Work norms
- Shared values
- The organization's uniqueness
- Communication
- Return on investment
- Recruitment and retention
- Employee motivation
- Organizational survival.

Defining Culture 1

Culture is an elusive concept for many organizations and their leaders. It seems that everyone has his or her own definition of this concept. Steven McShane and Mary Ann Von Glinow in *Organizational Behavior* provide a comprehensive definition of organizational culture:

"It is the basic pattern of shared assumptions, values and beliefs governing the way employees within an organization think about and act on problems and opportunities ... It (culture) defines what is important and unimportant in the company. You might think of it as the organization's DNA — invisible to the naked eye, yet a powerful template that shapes what happens in the workplace."

The definition helps frame the importance of culture. We often cannot see or sometimes totally describe all of the aspects of culture. Many of us take a simplistic approach and describe culture "as the way things are done around here." To help answer the burning question of "What is Culture?," Figure 3 identifies elements and behavioral aspects that we often attach to culture. These attributes help us understand how culture dramatically impacts an organization.

Values are at the top of the list in Figure 3 because it is easy for an organization to publish values that do not necessarily represent the culture. Espoused values are those publicly announced values that were mentioned in the Introduction. The real values are harder to define and must be shared by all members of the organization. A good example of a shared value is to place a high value on learning. In looking closer, this value encourages the development of all staff members and indicates a "learning culture." This learning culture must be reinforced with programs and actions that in fact support this shared value. Some total rewards programs that would support a learning culture include tuition reimbursement programs for all employees, generous continuing education programs, on-site corporate universities and pay-for-knowledge incentives. Shared values are a critical cultural driver because they help give meaning and shape to the organization. When an organization begins building its long-term strategy, it is the shared

FIGURE 3 Components of Culture

- **Values** — Espoused versus Shared
- **Norms** — Organizational versus Group
- **Leadership** — Formal versus Informal
- **Patterns of Behavior** — Individual versus Group
- **Communication Style** — Open versus Closed
- **Beliefs and Rituals** — Defined versus Hidden
- **Mission** — Espoused versus Enacted
- **Cultural Sensitivity** — High versus Low Level of Awareness
- **Diversity** — Representative versus Controlled
- **Formality** — Formal versus Informal
- **Innovation** — Encouraged versus Discouraged

values that will help develop a successful strategy. Many leaders forget about culture as an important element in helping define an organization's strategy.

This explains in part some of the devastating outcomes that have befallen large organizations in the past five years. Norms help frame the organization's culture. There are two types of norms. There are organizational and group norms. The organizational norms are those behaviors either formally defined or strongly encouraged by the organization. Some of these defined or highly encouraged norms can lead to negative consequences for the organization's culture. For example, even though an organization has a published attendance policy, if it is not uniformly administered, the culture will soon accept poor attendance as the norm. Group norms also impact the culture. This is a norm followed by the work team in the daily operations of the organization. Group A, for example, may have a norm in which all group members must contribute equally in the workload. Being ostracized by the rest of the group members is the result for those who fail to contribute their fair share.

Group norms can produce "cultural shock" for new employees. The group norms may be different than what the employee understood about the organization when they accepted the job. Figure 4 provides examples of positive and negative norms. It is interesting to note that if left alone, negative norms will develop and become the basis for the culture.

FIGURE 4 Positive Versus Negative Norms

Positive Norms	Negative Norms
• The organization rewards employees for providing excellent customer service. Note: Customer service is a major component of the performance evaluation system.	• It does not matter what you do around here; nobody cares anyway. Note: There is an absence of any formal employee-recognition program or informal recognition approaches.
• Employees are encouraged to participate in developing new ideas and programs. Note: A well-designed suggestion program reinforces this.	• The bottom line is more important than quality or service. Note: Leadership of the organization places very little value on quality or service.
• Employees are expected to keep their skill levels at a high level. Note: This is supported by a performance-incentive plan.	• Leaders are not held to the same level of performance standards as regular employees. Note: Individuals in leadership roles are conspicuously absent or unavailable to their employees.
• All employees will be free from harassment of any kind. Note: The organization has adopted a code of conduct for all employees.	Feeling of trust and fairness is violated — leaders' "Talk and Walk" not the same.

Action Point

Figure 4 provides examples of how to reinforce positive norms. What happens if leaders have no desire to provide total rewards programs to create positive work norms? The role of the HR practitioner is to make the "business case" for offering new total rewards programs. One of the cultural drivers is return on investment. This is part of the business case. The HR practitioner must show how offering new "culturally fit" programs will positively impact the bottom line and the success of the organization. This business case must show in dollars and cents how the new program reduces turnover, improves morale or improves productivity. Few managers are wedded to providing new programs to build a positive culture unless it can be proved that it will somehow help the organization financially grow or survive. This is a real challenge that HR practitioners face when introducing a new "culture friendly" program. The business case is enhanced if we can use benchmark data or "success stories" to illustrate how cultural enhancements have been successful in other organizations. A major resource is *Fortune's* annual "100 Best Companies to Work For." This publication includes examples of how successful companies have employed culture friendly approaches with resounding results.

Leadership is defined by culture. For example, if the culture values employees, leaders will generally value their employees. Leadership is the cultural driver that helps establish what direction the culture will follow. This direction may have positive or negative outcomes for the organization. Some organizational cultures do not have the benefit of having one leader to provide this direction. There is a big gap between managers and leaders. Figure 5 provides a comparison between what managers typically do and what leaders provide. The list provided in Figure 5 can be argued by management practitioners. It is meant as a tool to help differentiate the importance of looking at the difference between managers and leaders. The emphasis for the manager is on taking action while the leader seeks to provide "shared vision." Leaders know the importance of involving their followers in establishing the organization's vision and shaping its culture. For example, managers rely on their position's power to make decisions. Leaders empower employees to come up with a better decision.

Action Point

What happens when a manager refuses to let employees be involved in shaping the culture? This is often a reality that HR practitioners must face. Some potential tips for dealing with this issue are:

1. Utilize the subcultures within the organization. According to McShane and Von Glinow, "subcultures are located throughout (an organization's) divisions, geographic locations and occupational groups." HR can tap these subcultures to help improve morale and obtain the benefits of having a unified culture. By focusing on each subculture, HR can focus its resources on the employees contained within the subculture.

FIGURE 5 Comparison of Leaders and Managers

Leaders	Managers
• Shapes Culture	• Reacts to the Culture
• Aligns People to the Culture	• Seeks to Protect the Existing Culture
• Empowers Others	• Uses Position's Power
• Creates Shared Vision	• Provides Limited Options
• Future Oriented	• Oriented to the Present
• Proactive	• Reactive
• Seeks Consensus	• Seeks Compliance
• Serves or Stewards Followers	• Directs Others
• Focuses on What Decisions Mean to Others	• Focuses on How to Get Things Done
• Motivates and Inspires	• Controls and Monitors Results
• Creates Shared Solutions	• Fixes Problems

2. Present feedback from cultural audits and surveys to top management. This at least gives top management data about what is really important to employees. What they choose to do with this information can not always be predicted. It is HR's role to be an employee advocate and provide feedback so management is kept informed.

3. Provide "best practices" information about culture to management. Again, this can take many forms and must be carefully communicated. Still, it keeps culture in front of top management as an issue to consider.

4. Integrate culture within the HR strategy. Culture should be part of the HR strategy that is communicated to top management and to employees. It tells executive leadership that HR views culture as important to the organization's success.

5. Conduct training or information sessions with all levels of management about the importance of culture. HR should make a concerted effort to discuss the importance of culture with all management levels. The sessions can be 20 to 30 minutes initially. The trick is to get management involved with culture as a topic.

6. Seek out an executive champion. Identify an individual on the executive team who will be a spokesperson for the importance of culture to the organization. Finding someone on the executive team to do this takes patience and a willingness to teach this individual all about culture as an important organizational component.

Leaders energize, motivate and inspire their followers. Managers monitor results, plan for and prioritize problems and ensure proper staffing. An organization needs leaders and managers. Some individuals are good at being leaders and daily operational managers. However, if there is an absence of one or the other, the culture will be dramatically impacted. Leaders *align* people so the culture can be allowed to develop. Managers, however, *protect* the existing culture and ensure it can survive and be successful. This seems straightforward for the formal side of leadership. But the informal leader can have just as big of an impact on the culture. Who are these informal leaders? Informal leaders are those individuals to whom employees look for support and approval.

Informal leaders do not have the title of manager or supervisor but still employees see them as important to the culture. Smart organizations know the importance of the informal leader and will voluntarily involve them in the decision-making process.

Informal leaders help feed the grapevine by giving employees information — negative and positive — about the organization. The result can be devastating when making change or merging cultures. Without accurate information, informal leaders may fill in the blanks based on their perceptions, personal values and needs of their work group. An informal leader can be a friend or mighty foe to how the culture develops and how it continues to be communicated. Bottom line: Identify these leaders and involve them as much as possible.

Discussion Point

In many instances, the informal leader is the "keeper" of the subculture. The informal leader may have defined or helped form the subculture for the individual department, unit or division. This individual is key to determining what employees really view as valuable and important to their world. Informal leaders should have as much information as possible about changes that will impact the organization. This is not a move to manipulate the informal leader but a proactive step in developing an overall culture that more accurately reflects the needs of the employee. Feedback from informal leaders should be scrutinized and shared with executive leadership unless the informal leader does not want her/his feedback "shared up the ladder." Even when this happens, the feedback can be important to improve the work life of the employees in that department or division. Managers must nurture the informal leader and make him/her a part of the process in managing and assessing the organization's culture.

Patterns of behavior also determine how the culture develops. Do we strive for an organization based on individual accomplishments and contributions? Or do we seek a culture based on group behavior and group achievements? There really is no right answer. The reality is most organizations are driven by individual and group behavior. In fact, we reward employees for their individual and team accomplishments. Patterns of behavior can be extremely negative on a team basis. Teams may have difficulties working together and sharing the workload. "Social loafing" can be the consequence when all team members do not contribute equally. The social loafer piggybacks on the accomplishments of the team. The reaction can be outrage by the rest of the team and force negative patterns of behavior. Some individuals are committed to the organization's success. This individual pattern of behavior can be contagious, particularly if this individual is rewarded for her/his contributions. Conversely, "one bad apple" does seem to spoil the whole bunch. Individuals who display negative patterns of behavior, if left unchecked, can erode a positive organizational structure.

The big takeaway is to harness positive patterns of work behavior and incorporate them into the culture and work environment. The communication style of an organization may be open or closed. Figure 6 provides an excellent graphic of how the two styles work. Communication flows two ways in an open communication culture. Looking closely, it resembles an endless circle with continuous feedback and communication. The closed communication style is one-way, top-down and filtered and controlled by organizational leadership. An uptight culture is often built around the closed style of communication. In the absence of accurate communication, employees will fill in the blanks. That generally produces negative results. A good example is how the closed organization communicates salary information. It is carefully guarded with only a few individuals privy to how the compensation system works. While this may sound absolutely necessary to managers of the organization, a leader knows the value of sharing basic information about the compensation system. Once it is fully understood by employees, the compensation system can be seen as a valuable component of the employee's work life. Without this knowledge, employees may feel the system is inequitable and unfair.

Discussion Point

How do you survive in an organization that practices a closed communication style? Many organizations are "tight-lipped." To survive in this type of organization, managers must create "an alternative reality." This alternative reality focuses on the needs of the subculture and how to best communicate with the employees. It means the manager must actively share information that he/she knows is accurate. Subculture must focus on open communication to be effective and productive. This is where the manager can be most valuable. The byline for this approach is: "Focus on what you have control over." Most managers have more control over the flow of communication within their subculture rather than the culture as a whole. Do not advocate being insubordinate or refusing to work within the boundaries established by the overall culture. Instead, utilize the informal leaders and employees within the subculture to create an open and positive communication approach. Start this by having frequent department/unit meetings where open communication is encouraged and practiced. If there is a geographic separation, open communication should be practiced virtually as well as in person. In a virtual setting, the use of "employee chat rooms" and "hotlines" should be encouraged. Keep in mind this approach should not be subversive but as an adjunct to the overall culture that unfortunately practices a closed approach to communication. It is useful to model an open approach to communication with employees and colleagues when working in a closed environment to set an inviting tone.

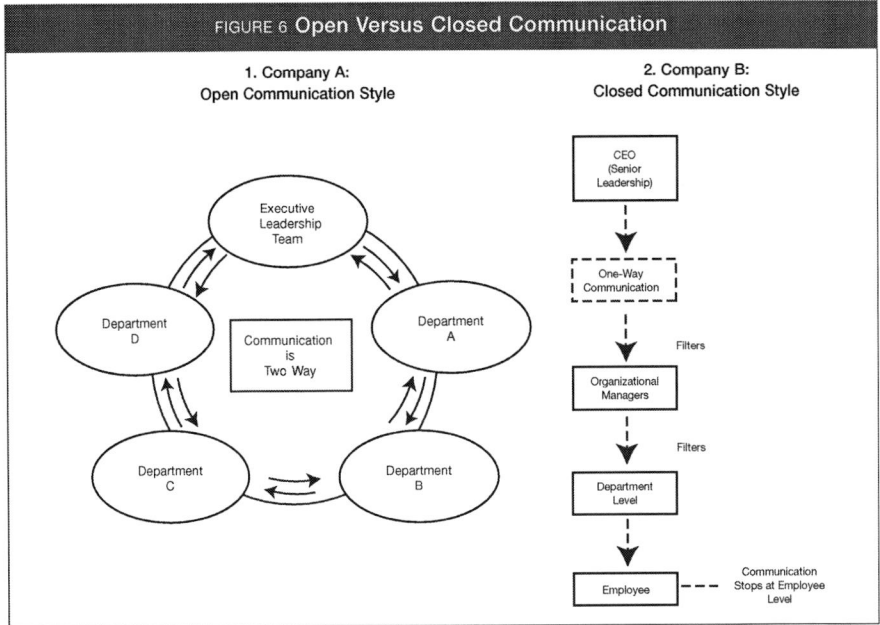

FIGURE 6 **Open Versus Closed Communication**

Beliefs and rituals can be defined or hidden within the culture. A service award program, which recognized employees with long-term service, is an example of defined beliefs and rituals. An example of a hidden belief or ritual is how employees are encouraged to interact with one another and with the organization's external customers. This hidden ritual can help create a caring and responsive culture. If employees are empowered to resolve customer issues on the spot, it can result in a positive impact on customer relations.

The espoused mission (i.e., the written mission hanging on the wall) needs to be absorbed into the culture if it is to have any meaning. Often, it is the enacted mission that drives the organization's culture. For example, if the mission states "we strive to deliver timely and courteous service to our customers" and the organization instead regularly mistreats its customers and rarely delivers anything on time, the organization is functioning at a different mindset than what it is actively communicating to its employees and customers. The mission can be a driving force for the culture or a useless statement that some "management geek" made up to appease the public.

Cultural sensitivity and diversity will be discussed at length in Chapter 2. However, it is important to note that these two concepts have a behavioral impact on the organization's culture. If an organization is tuned into how differences can work to the advantage of the organization, a richer and more representative culture can result. Organizations with very little commitment to "equal employment opportunity," or honoring the heritages and backgrounds of their employees, produce controlled cultures incapable of adapting to change or crisis. Trust also intertwines with diversity and cultural sensitivity. Employees will develop a high level of trust when the organization is committed to serving and stewarding them rather than controlling their work habits.

This concept is vital to how the culture leads or manages its employees. Figure 5 identified stewardship as an important leadership component. The servant or steward leader builds trust because she/he helps her/his followers succeed. A "trust gap" develops when the leader or the organization is not sensitive to the needs of his/her or its followers and employees. An organization that hides information or fails to provide appropriate resources, rewards and compensation levels to its employees produces a trust gap that is difficult to overcome.

The final two components of culture are greatly impacted by one another. Formality refers to how the organization is structured. For example, is the organization very formal with well-defined policies and procedures along with a very definitive organization hierarchy? On the other hand, is the organization loosely organized with very little dependence on formal structure, policies or practices?

Formality generally impacts how innovation is incorporated into its culture. A very formal structure may discourage innovation if it changes the "status quo." An informal organization may be more open to innovation and new ideas because it generally relies more on change because formal policies and practices are not well entrenched in the organization. Formality and innovation define how the culture can adapt and adopt new ideas and changes. Formal organizations are generally slower to adapt than informal organizations. Organizations driven by innovation and creative ideas are more apt to provide total rewards programs that reinforce this commitment. If innovation is eschewed by the organization, the culture will be more controlled and stagnant.

Importance of Culture

Culture provides direction to the organization and its members by influencing behavior so organizational goals and strategies can be accomplished. The degree with which culture is shared will determine if it has a significant impact on the organization. Figure 7 identifies characteristics of a shared and closed culture. Notice that the most important element of a shared culture is the pervasiveness and degree it is accepted. According to Professor Richard Scholl of the University of Rhode Island, pervasiveness is an extremely important cultural attribute because it indicates the culture has widespread acceptance and identity.

Discussion Point

The concept of "shared" and "closed" cultures is not meant to be a value judgment but to point out the importance of having a shared culture. If the culture is not shared, it obviously will have less impact and importance. Many organizations have closed cultures with a "top down" approach to managing. This "top down" approach is a real concern for some managers and one they must try to reconcile with their own management beliefs. For others, the closed culture works and "fits" with the leadership styles of their organization. This style is not as effective as a shared culture

> **FIGURE 7 Attributes of Shared and Closed Cultures**
>
> **Shared Cultures Are:**
>
> - **Pervasive**
>   Culture is widely shared among the organization.
> - **Accepted**
>   Culture is widely accepted and valued by organizational members.
> - **Diverse**
>   Composition is representative of various cultures and beliefs.
> - **Adaptable**
>   Has the ability to adapt to change and address crises.
> - **Encouraging**
>   Encourages organizational members to do their best.
> - **Driven by Outcomes**
>   Focus on goals and strategies.
> - **Cooperative**
>   Organizational members work well together.
> - **Strategic**
>   Focus on the future success of the organization.
> - **Innovative**
>   Creativity and risk taking are valued.
> - **Customer Focused**
>   Internal and external customers are valued.
> - **Identity Based**
>   Provides a positive identity to its members.
>
> **Closed Cultures Are:**
>
> - **Disjointed**
>   There is not a system of shared values and beliefs.
> - **Controlled**
>   New ideas are not valued. Organizational make-up is not representative of the external environment.
> - **Competitive**
>   Individual achievement displaces cooperation and team spirit.
> - **Cost Focused**
>   The bottom line is more important than people.
> - **Process Based**
>   Current processes are maintained at the expense of creativity and innovation.
> - **Driven by Daily Routine**
>   There is very little attention given to strategic planning.
> - **Ambiguous**
>   There are no goals or strategies to drive the organization.

because it relies more on control rather than active communication and proactive results. Both of these concepts are presented in the hopes the reader will carefully review those contained within a shared culture.

Shared cultures focus on strategic planning, people and the future. Closed cultures pay more attention to protecting the status quo. The importance of culture is fairly obvious from reviewing these attributes. It is the foundation from which to build a successful organization. This foundation determines how to:

1. **Frame Organizational Strategy:** This is impacted by how open the culture is to adapting to change and new ideas. It is virtually impossible to implement strategy that focuses on growth if the culture is driven by daily operations.
2. **Build Organizational Success:** A strong culture is the driver for the organization's success. Strong cultures already have mechanisms in place to solidify financial and customer success. These mechanisms include a strong customer focus, cooperative and diverse teams, and the ability to adapt to new ideas and change.
3. **Grow Adaptive Organizational Members:** Strong cultures focus on team spirit and cooperativeness. Strong cultures are also driven by creativity and innovation. This innovative spirit motivates employees to learn, contribute and achieve. Employees who are encouraged to learn and contribute are more open to strategic change. Organizations are sometimes surprised that their employees are intimidated by change. A closer look generally reveals that the organization's culture does not encourage new ways of doing things. One example of a total rewards program that may help build a status quo culture is "automatic salary adjustments" which are not tied to performance or contribution.

Finally, culture has a dramatic impact on individual and group behavior. How organizational members embrace the culture will determine its impact. Shared cultures generally have highly visible leaders. Those leaders help mold the culture so it has a high level of support from its key stakeholders. The biggest impact that leaders have on culture is to provide a strong role model for its followers. If the leader can provide a cultural connection by being a positive role model, followers will be more committed to the culture and to the organization. For some leaders, like former General Electric chief executive officer, Jack Welch, this identification with the culture can encompass the organization. Some leaders are so identified with the culture that it is hard for followers to separate the two. This is why it is important to "walk the talk" and provide a positive image for followers.

Matching Culture with Strategic Goals

Figure 8 provides a checklist that can be used to integrate culture with strategy. Not surprisingly, this checklist begins with leadership. The other five components in the checklist build on leadership and how the organization responds to each cultural area.

Leaders of an organization must keep well informed about the culture and how it impacts strategy. For example, how would culture impact the following strategy, which relates to organizational integration?

Strategy
Create a single operation and point of contact for key support functions to improve efficiency and reduce costs.

FIGURE 8 Checklist for Integrating Culture with Strategy

1. **Leadership**
    - ☐ Must be team oriented, well informed and knowledgeable of the culture.
    - ☐ Must be open to suggestions, concerns and "insights" about how culture can impact organizational strategy.

2. **Strategy**
    - ☐ Must be clear and specific with few written goals.
    - ☐ Is relevant to cultural issues and capable of dealing with any problems as they arise.
    - ☐ Should reflect the impact of the organization's culture on the organization's success.
    - ☐ Integrates cultural preferences with the capabilities of the organization.

3. **Climate**
    - ☐ Must be open to new strategic approaches.
    - ☐ Must demonstrate a willingness to accept change.
    - ☐ Should align positively with the culture and the strategy.

4. **Communication**
    - ☐ Provides extensive feedback opportunities.
    - ☐ Sends positive and proactive messages to organizational members.
    - ☐ Feeds the grapevine with accurate information.
    - ☐ Enriches the cultural beliefs and values.

5. **Culture**
    - ☐ Determines if strategy is a "fit" for the organization.
    - ☐ Establishes prevailing attitudes regarding strategy.
    - ☐ Must be aligned with the strategy.
    - ☐ Encourages support and acceptance of the strategy.

6. **Training and Development**
    - ☐ Seeks to match culture with the strategy.
    - ☐ Enlightens stakeholders about the strategy.
    - ☐ Provides an unbiased source for learning about strategic planning process.

The leaders of this organization better have a good idea of how the culture will support such a lofty goal. This strategy, in effect, changes the organization from a decentralized to a centralized operation. This strategy will change how decisions are made within the organization. Key questions for leadership in this example would include:

1. Can the culture support a change from a decentralized to a centralized organizational structure?
2. Will key stakeholders understand the need to make this change?
3. Why is this change needed in the first place?
4. How can this change be effectively communicated to key stakeholders?
5. Is the organizational climate willing to support this change?
6. Will other initiatives impact the success of this strategy?
7. Does this strategy fit with what the culture has traditionally deemed to be important?
8. What training and development will key stakeholders need before this strategy can be implemented?

If the culture focused on empowering employees and allowing decision-making at the department level, it will be difficult to implement this strategy. Strategy simply cannot be forced with any degree of great success when it contradicts tradition and culture. To be successful, organizations must ensure that the strategy is a good fit for the culture *before* making dramatic shifts in strategic direction.

Impact of Culture on Total Rewards Programs

Figure 9 details how total rewards programs are culturally driven. The bottom half of the circle graph delineates programs aimed at "work-life strategies." These programs are driven by the intrinsic needs of the employee. All employees have personal needs that are distinguished from their basic financial needs. To address those needs, organizations must offer work-life programs that help employees cope with their personal lives and the daily grind of the workplace. Some of these programs include:

Shared Culture: Employees who work for an organization that has a shared culture have a distinct advantage over those individuals stuck in a closed one. Shared cultures are well defined and widely communicated, and that positions the organization when developing strategy and making changes. Employees generally are more confident about their work experience when the culture is in sync with their personal values and beliefs.

Flexible Scheduling: These programs provide opportunities for employees to match their work schedules with their personal needs. Job *sharing* is a type of flexible scheduling arrangement where two or more employees share a full-time position. The individuals who share the position are empowered to take responsibility for staffing it. Job sharing has produced outstanding results in the insurance, retail and health-care fields. *Telecommuting* provides another flexible approach that allows employees to work from home. This is accomplished with the aid of microcomputers and other technological devices. It has spawned the concept of "virtual teams." These teams are

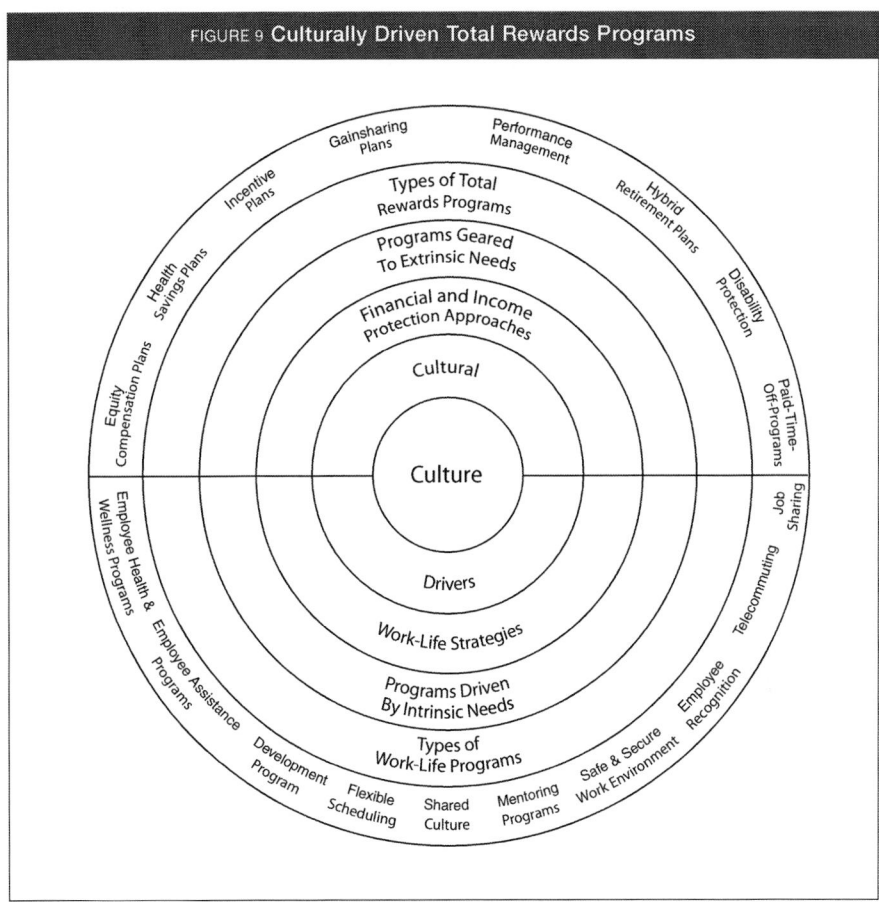

FIGURE 9 **Culturally Driven Total Rewards Programs**

comprised of telecommuters and may include participants in remote or global locations. These teams provide unique work-life benefits. However, they offer some unique challenges to organizations in effectively managing them.

Employee Recognition: Recognizing employees for a job well done is an important component of the total rewards strategy. Employee recognition programs can range from formal, which provide monetary incentives, to very informal, which provide on-the-spot recognition. Employee recognition programs can also be used to focus the culture on a strategic goal. One such example is a recognition program that places a high value on providing excellent customer service. This program helps the employee focus on the customer, which ultimately can create a "customer-friendly culture."

Development Programs: These programs provide training to employees and other key stakeholders. Some organizations have created on-site, corporate universities for the convenience of their employees. Mentoring programs that place experienced employees with new employees have become widely accepted. Mentoring is more than on-the-job training. It allows the new employee to be indoctrinated into the organization's culture. The new employee has a seasoned resource at the ready to offer advice, training and initial orientation. Some of these mentoring relationships become long lasting. Organizations with a high commitment to training and development can build a learning culture that values new ideas and creativity.

Employee Health and Wellness: These programs focus on healthy lifestyles and disease prevention. Cultures placing a high value on health and wellness know the value of taking care of the total employee. Obviously, a healthy employee is generally more productive, happier and more positive about their work experience. Some examples of health and wellness programs include on-site fitness centers and employee health functions, health counseling programs, employee health fairs and weight-loss programs. To address stress and other personal problems, some organizations offer employee assistance programs to provide counseling services to the employee and their family members. These services are generally provided off-site and in a confidential setting. Finally, providing a safe and secure work environment free of workplace injuries and violence has become a major challenge to employers. According to the National Institute for Occupational Safety and Health (NIOSH), at least one million employees are victims of workplace violence annually with at least 1,000 of these cases resulting in homicides. According to statistics maintained by the Occupational Safety and Health Administration (OSHA), workplace homicides are the leading cause of fatal occupational injuries for women and the second leading cause for men. This difficult problem has been exacerbated by the potential threat of terrorism since the Sept. 11, 2001, terrorist attacks. Employee accidents represent another major risk factor for employers. Most organizations have a safety committee or safety officer who monitors unsafe work practices and develops in-house safety programs.

The aforementioned list of work-life programs is not exhaustive. Many organizations continue to devise unique ways to enhance the employee's work experience. For example, J.M. Smucker, *Fortune's* "Best Company to Work For" in 2004, serves complimentary bagels and muffins complete with its signature jams to its employees on a daily basis. Smucker's goal is to create a "family-oriented" culture. The financial and income-protection approaches identified in the top half of Figure 9 should complement the work-life strategies. Financial and income-protection approaches focus on the "extrinsic needs" of the employee. These programs "pay the bills." Figure 9 identified only a few, although countless compensation and employee benefits programs exist. Looking at this vast number is beyond the scope of this book. Instead, let's focus on the following three approaches:

1. **Performance Management:** These programs provide monetary rewards for meeting certain defined performance criteria. A merit performance program is the most common approach. It rewards employees for achieving varying levels of

work performance (e.g., Outstanding — 7 percent, Very Effective — 5 percent, and Effective — 3 percent). The problem with this approach is that it generally fails to produce a positive impact on the culture. For a performance management program to be linked to the culture, it must reward those factors, which are most significant to its success. For example, rewarding specific behaviors for customer service links it to the culture, as opposed to arbitrarily checking some vague measures on a fixed performance scale. A "culturally anchored evaluation" relies heavily on the leader's involvement in observing the employee performing certain highly valued behaviors. Figure 10 compares a traditional way of evaluating customer relations skills to a culturally anchored approach.

In Figure 10, the focus is on building positive work behaviors. The result is to reward and reinforce behavior that will lead to the development of a "customer-friendly" culture. Those individuals who do not embrace these behaviors will generally self-select out of the organization.

2. **Incentive Plans:** The goal of an incentive plan is to provide a structured schedule for rewarding certain individual or group performance. From a cultural perspective, incentives should also reinforce behavior and performance, which matches the organization's strategic direction. Some examples of culturally designed incentives include:

- *Cultural-Sharing Plans:* Incentive bonuses are paid based on the quality, service and financial performance of the organization. Cultural-sharing plans are similar to gainsharing plans that share some of the revenue gains with employees. The major difference between the two types of approaches is that cultural-sharing plans seek to link strategy and culture with the incentive. Specific improvements in quality, service and value are drivers for these culturally based incentives. If customer service, for example, improves the other two elements are generally impacted and vice versa. The cultural-sharing plan establishes specific trigger points (i.e., increased customer service scores, fewer product returns, community-based involvement) to reward employees. If these factors are effectively reinforced, the bottom line will be positively impacted and the image of the organization in the community will be enhanced.

- *Group Cultural Incentives:* These incentives are based on organizational units (e.g., marketing, financial services, sales, production, etc.) achieving certain culturally related goals. Some examples of these departmental contributions would include increasing customer relations scores; reducing departmental turnover rates; developing new work processes or improving existing ones; improving service turnaround times; or developing new quality and service initiatives.

- Individual Incentives: These incentives are based on verifiable contributions of the individual employee to the organization. Some examples of

FIGURE 10 Traditional Versus Culturally Anchored Performance Evaluation

Example: Evaluating Customer Relations Skills

Traditional Evaluation Approach	Culturally Anchored Approach
1. **Evaluation Instructions:** Evaluate the employee on his or her customer relations skills using the following rating scale. Check only one rating level.	1. **Evaluation Instructions:** Evaluate the employee on the following cultural aspects regarding customer service. Check all that apply.
2. **Performance Rating Scale:** ☐ OUTSTANDING: Performs at the highest levels. ☐ VERY EFFECTIVE: Performance is performed in a competent manner with few examples of errors. ☐ EFFECTIVE: Performance is adequate and acceptable. ☐ MINIMALLY SATISFACTORY: Performance is marginal and fails to meet standards. ☐ UNSATISFACTORY: A deadline for improvement must be established or the employee will be terminated.	2. **Cultural Contributions:** ☐ Enhances and enriches the culture when delivering customer service. Provide examples: _____ ☐ Has made one or more contributions to the success of the team in the past quarter. Identify contributions: _____ ☐ Received one or more compliments from customers regarding service delivery. Provide examples: _____ ☐ Successfully resolved at least one customer concern in the last three months. Detail problem(s) resolved: _____

contributions to the culture might include the enhancement of the individual employee's job skills; the employee successfully completes a critical competency-based training program; the employee takes the lead in developing new programs or approaches that will positively impact the organization's culture; and the employee suggests new ideas or processes that contribute to the financial success of the organization. The purpose of the individual incentive is to reward contributions that enhance the culture and the organization's strategy.

3. **Hybrid Retirement Plans:** Cultural-driven rewards programs should adapt to the unique needs of employees. Income-protection plans, which focus on such areas as retirement, health coverage and disability protection, can be customized to meet these unique expectations of the culture. One such example is a cash balance retirement plan. This hybrid retirement approach bases benefits on the career average earnings of the employee. This type of retirement plan is perfect for those organizations, which have a younger workforce. Cash balance plans are more portable than a traditional retirement plan and can be paid out in a lump sum when the employee leaves. This is extremely attractive to the younger employee who wants to build his or her career without staying in one place. Traditional defined benefit plans place more weight on the last five or 10 years of employment when paying out benefits. However, organizations that have a preponderance of long-term employees would *not* want to eliminate defined benefit plans in favor of a cash balance approach. Long-term employees are better off having a defined benefit plan because its value increases as the employee ages. Takeaway: Offer benefit plans geared to the employee's needs, age, service tenure and income levels. A well-designed benefits program can enhance the culture by providing employees with a sense of security and belonging.

The organization's total rewards programs can make or break the company's "cultural reputation." The Container Store, a previous "Best Company to Work For," provides health insurance coverage to everyone who works at least 18 hours or more a week. The Container Store understands the importance of providing health coverage to lower-paid retail employees. The result has been lower employee turnover and a dramatic commitment to the organization's culture and mission.

Figure 9 has the cultural drivers surrounding the culture. The purpose is to illustrate the importance of how culture drives the organization's success. Having a diverse culture representative of the area that the organization serves is one of the more important drivers. How diversity impacts the culture is a significant driver when developing the organization's strategy. The next chapter will discuss the importance of this cultural driver.

Cultural Diversity 2

Individuals enter the workplace with unique perspectives shaped by their interactions, personal beliefs and experiences. This uniqueness contributes to developing a diverse workplace culture. The traditional hierarchical, white-male dominated environment is no longer the norm. In fact, one out of four people in the workforce are African American, Hispanic or Asian American. Women account for 63 percent of the new entrants into the workforce. There are more people older than age 65 than teenagers. The bottom line is the workplace has become a "melting pot" for diversity.

Figure 11 identifies the "4 Ps" of diversity. These four factors are instrumental in determining if diversity is a positive or negative element for the organization's culture.

FIGURE 11 4 Ps of Diversity

- Perception
- Politics
- Perspective
- Process

Perception

An organization can build a *negative perception* that it does not value diversity. Some examples of organizational behavior that can result in a negative perception include:

- Practicing highly selective employment practices
- Offering only "traditional" employee benefits
- Creating a homogeneous work environment comprised of few minorities and individuals from similar cultural backgrounds
- Creating policies and procedures that are discriminatory in favor of certain individuals.

Politics

Politics inside and outside of an organization often determine the composition of the work environment. The political outlook from within the organization regarding diversity establishes the cultural tone. Leaders who are unwilling to embrace the advantages of diversity can stilt this political outlook. A negative outlook becomes

> **Case Study: First Horizon National Bank**
>
> Organizations that value differences do so by building a diverse culture on openness and equality. One example is First Horizon National Bank, which actively promotes women into manager roles. First Horizon also gives employees with children unlimited time to visit their kids' classrooms. Obviously, First Horizon has built a positive perception as an equal opportunity employer. How the business uses its organizational learning to shape the perception of diversity is extremely important. Organizational learning includes how knowledge is imparted to employees and to key stakeholders within the community. First Horizon has chosen to shape this perception by supplementing its beliefs with a positive work-life program. This, in turn, has a positive impact on what is learned about the organization. If the approach is positive, the impact is long standing and permanently imprinted on the culture.

apparent to even outsiders who notice that the culture is "controlled and structured." By applying politics internally, the organization seeks to maintain the status quo. In this instance, the "good old boy" or "good old girl" network may dominate the political outlook.

This may result in:

- Hiring individuals who have training or educational degrees from specific schools or universities
- Placing culturally diverse individuals in meaningless roles or offering them few advancement opportunities
- Centering organizational control and decision making with a few select cliques or individuals
- Creating a personality profile that others must meet to be successful. (Note: This results in valuing certain physical and personal attributes. A good example is promoting only tall, white, athletic males to leadership positions.)

Politics from the outside of the organization can be much more subtle and difficult to pinpoint. Some examples might include:

- Valuing certain relationships within a geographical location (e.g., personal relationships, relatives, "native son/daughter," personal ties to an individual, property ownership)
- Restricting access to community organizations based on selective criteria (e.g., race, gender, appearance, social status, etc.)
- Having a low tolerance for diversity (e.g., the community in which the organization is located)
- Not encouraging or protecting workplace diversity (e.g., the local and state laws in the regional area)

- Having a low tolerance for diversity (e.g., the community in which the organization is located)
- Not encouraging or protecting workplace diversity (e.g., the local and state laws in the regional area).

Perspective

The organization's perspective determines if diversity will be practiced. Perspective is accompanied by the thought that each organizational culture believes it is superior. By bringing in "undesirables" from the outside, this superiority belief could be destroyed.

This belief of superiority, and feeling of contempt of other groups and cultures, is called *ethnocentrism*. Ethnocentrism is the result of overvaluing one's way of life, while devaluing others. An organization can reduce ethnocentrism through:

- *Increased awareness.* Talking about diversity openly and frankly
- *Education.* The organization can educate its members about diversity. This type of training can help organizational members replace old stereotypes with new information about the diverse individuals.
- *Evaluation of old and new information.* Once employees obtain new sources of information, they can then more effectively evaluate and decide which views to let go of, which to hold on to and which to add to their personal belief system regarding diversity.

A negative perspective can be changed and replaced with understanding and acceptance. To change perspective, the organization and its leaders must be willing to break down barriers and destroy outdated stereotypes. This can be done by positively communicating respect for all people and cultures to organizational members.

Process

The process is the final "P" that can dramatically impact how diversity will be absorbed into the culture. The diversity process is the organization's strategy for incorporating diversity into the culture. To fully embrace the diversity process, the organization must answer this time-sensitive question: Why does diversity matter? (See Figure 12.)

Workplace diversity should help create an all-inclusive environment where divergent skills, cultural perspectives and ethnic backgrounds are valued. When this happens, there are many benefits for the organization. Figure 12 lists some of these benefits and helps answer the diversity question. The diversity process helps the organization achieve better outcomes for its employees, customers and shareholders/stakeholders. By harnessing the brightest and most talented individuals, without regard to stereotypes or profiles, the organization is making a

> **FIGURE 12 Why Diversity Matters**
>
> - Helps the organization work with changing demographics
> - Improves interpersonal relationships
> - Makes the organization more productive and successful
> - Enhances synergy and teamwork
> - Complies with federal law and other regulatory guidelines
> - Prevents high turnover of talented employees
> - Enhances the organization's ability to communicate effectively
> - Helps build a learning organization
> - Improves morale and job satisfaction
> - Values all employees equally
> - Helps attract new talent
> - Develops a positive reputation in the community
> - Eliminates strife and personal distractions at work
> - Improves service delivery by valuing all individuals
> - Provides unique perspectives
> - Takes advantage of the talent offered by diverse individuals.

commitment to diversity. Appendix A provides a template to build a workplace diversity strategy.

This template focuses on five goals for achieving diversity:

1. **Awareness.** How does one make employees and customers aware of the importance of workplace diversity?
2. **Work Practices.** What workplace programs should be put in place to support diversity?
3. **Monitoring and Evaluation.** What systems will be used to monitor and evaluate the success of the diversity program?
4. **Implementation.** What steps need to be implemented to establish the program?
5. **Organizational Actions.** What actions need to be taken to ensure that diversity is important to the organization?

Please take a few minutes and review the template and use it as a starting point for developing a strategy for your organization.

Diversity Factors

A number of factors impact cultural diversity. Figure 13 lists some of the more common factors. These factors can be broken down into two groups:

- **Primary Factors** — These are "immutable human differences that are inborn" and exert an early influence about how we view diverse individuals. Some of the common primary factors are:
  - Age
  - Ethnicity — the ethnic and cultural background of an individual
  - Gender
  - Race
  - Sexual Orientation
  - Personality
  - Physical Ability.

- **Secondary Factors** — These factors can be acquired, changed, discarded or modified over the course of an individual's life. Below are some examples:
  - Education
  - Appearance
  - Socioeconomic Status
  - Marital Status
  - Geographic Location
  - Work Experience
  - Religion/Religious Beliefs.

> **FIGURE 13 Diversity Factors That Impact Culture**
> - Work Experience
> - Geographic Location
> - Religion/Religious Beliefs
> - Marital Status
> - Socioeconomic Status
> - Education
> - Sexual Orientation
> - Physical Ability
> - Personality
> - Ethnicity
> - Race
> - Gender
> - Age

The primary factors often get the most attention when addressing diversity. This is because these factors are so ingrained in how we see and value others. This publication could dedicate a chapter to each of the primary factors. However, the focus will be to identify them and assess their impact on the culture.

The secondary factors are becoming more important to the culture. For example, the socioeconomic status of individuals often labels them as "the haves" and "the have nots" in the organization. This can be devastating to those individuals labeled as the "have nots." Religion has become a factor that can divide some organizations. It becomes a heavily contested topic around the water cooler. It has also become a "protected" factor by federal and state legislation. Geographic location produces interesting problems for organizational members. An organization may have different customs, beliefs and values based on where they are located. For example, hunting season may be a call to use temporary help in a southern location as employees rush to participate in one of their favorite pastimes. Finally, individuals bring different work experiences, training and education to the workplace. This produces new organizational knowledge and challenges to those who have been with the company for a while.

Figure 14 depicts some of the organizational elements of diversity. Each element has an impact on the employee's work experience. *Cultural content* refers to the commonly held beliefs and practices that the organization supports. They are enriched by the degree of cultural diversity present in the organization. One example of cultural content, and how it influences diversity, is an organization's practice of accommodating various religious and ethnic beliefs. Some organizations not only honor cultural differences but also encourage employees to share their beliefs with the rest of the workplace. For example, Alston & Bird, a law firm in Atlanta, tells employees to put families first. Alston & Bird tells employees "there is no pecking order mentality" in this organization.

The *political climate* establishes the level of acceptance of diversity. The *political outlook*, as previously discussed, helps form the basis for accepting diversity. A political climate that is unwilling to change its outlook regarding diversity will generally have a restricted environment. *Union affiliation* adds another culture for the organization to consider. The union is an outside source, which brings its own cultural beliefs to its members.

The importance of *leadership* and its influence on diversity has already been discussed. Leaders who are committed to diversity will see it as valuable to the organization. They support and create diverse work teams by ensuring the organization provides equal access for all employees.

The type of *job classifications* and *work content* contribute to the diverse make-up of the organization. For example, by focusing on diversity only for the lower-level jobs that require very few skills, the organization leaves the perception that diversity is a

FIGURE 14 Organizational Elements of Diversity

- Cultural Content
- Political Climate
- Union Affiliation
- Leadership Influence
- Job Classifications
- Work Content
- Subgroup Culture
- Seniority
- Compensation and Rewards Systems

"necessary evil" and does not apply to everyone in the workplace. A better approach is to provide job opportunities at all levels, which accentuate the skills and potential for everyone.

Each *subgroup, department* or *work area* has its own unique culture fueled by the members' individuality. Each subgroup culture further adds to workplace diversity. The influence by subgroups sometimes has a negative influence. Physicians and nurses are examples of how subgroup cultures can, at times, be at odds even when both groups have the same customers.

Seniority is such a definitive element in the workplace that it often creates two separate cultures. One culture is for the "long timers" who have valuable organizational knowledge but may be reluctant to share it. The second culture is built around "newcomers and short timers," who sometimes work for the smug long timers. The best alternative is to utilize the abilities of the two groups to create a common culture. Long timers can be used to mentor and develop the newcomers and short timers and share their valuable knowledge in a more positive and focused manner.

Finally, the organization's *compensation and rewards systems* must reinforce diversity by offering programs that reward the contributions of everyone. This can be accomplished by having well-defined systems that focus on measurable outcomes and accomplishments.

Integrating Diversity with Culture

Diversity and culture can be on a collision course unless the organization takes appropriate steps to fully integrate the two. Figure 15 provides the four key components for integrating culture and diversity: strategy, values, intergroup relationships and leadership styles.

Strategy

This is different than creating an independent diversity strategy such as the one provided in Appendix A. There needs to be an ongoing strategy, that supports and encourages diversity. This strategy should be specific and identify behaviors that are needed to support workplace diversity. If you cannot see, feel or

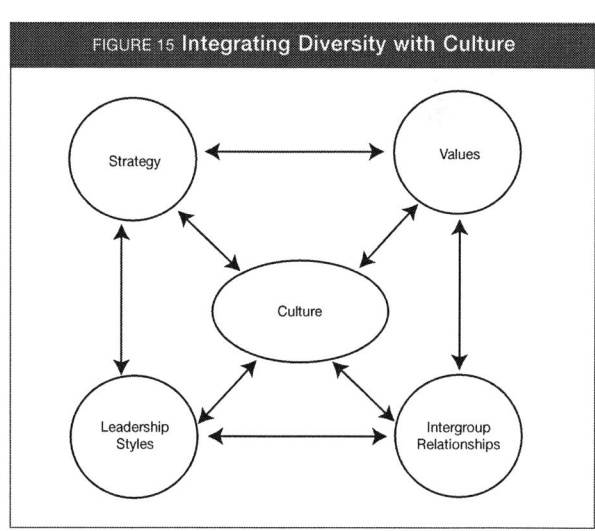

FIGURE 15 **Integrating Diversity with Culture**

measure it, diversity becomes an "invisible" strategy. For example, if the organization seeks to be more tolerant of all individuals, it must have a strategy for carrying out this practice. Let's look at how an organization might approach workplace tolerance.

Figure 16 provides an example of how an organization should focus on each element of its diversity program. The one missing component is the determination of who benefits from the changing behaviors and actions necessary to achieve workplace tolerance. Obviously, the entire organization ends up being better off by having a more tolerant workplace. However, the internal and external customers also benefit. Each of the changes in behaviors and actions listed in Figure 16 must have associated benefits before they will be accepted by the organization. For example, it sounds nice to be more open minded to others, but why should employees care? One benefit of being open minded is that it promotes team success. Employees working for a group incentive should be able to see that there is a financial advantage of being open minded even if the human element is lost on them.

FIGURE 16 Strategy for Workplace Tolerance

Goal

All individuals will be treated with dignity, respect and consideration regardless of ethnic background, gender, age, race or other unique quality.

Expected Outcomes

- More tolerant and accepting workplace
- Enhanced workplace communication
- Improved efficiencies and productivity
- More enriched and culturally diverse workplace.

Measures

- Improved job satisfaction as measured by the employee opinion survey
- Lower turnover of culturally diverse individuals
- A workplace comprised of individuals who are statistically representative of the area population
- Improved acceptance of others as determined by employee and customer feedback.

Changes in Behaviors/Actions

- Employees will be more open minded in their interactions with others.
- The organization will be free of harassment or discrimination of any kind.
- Employees will consistently display a willingness and commitment to treating others with respect and dignity.
- The organization must actively promote its successes in creating a more tolerant workplace.

Values

Diversity must be integrated into the values of the culture. This can be accomplished by inserting diversity into the cultural landscape. Some approaches to inserting diversity include displaying culturally diverse employees in organizational publications; making diversity an integral part of new employee orientation; providing an equal opportunity workplace and offering diversity training to all organizational members. The best way to incorporate diversity into the culture is to create an inclusive environment, valuing different perspectives, skills and backgrounds. Such an environment must practice employment equity in all of its daily operations. A valuable tool for modeling and protecting workplace diversity, employment equity ensures that all workplace decisions are based on merit and free from discrimination. Once employees see the organization is serious about valuing diversity, it will become a "self-fulfilling prophecy." Employees will then value diversity as important element of their own work experience.

Intergroup Relationships

Each work group within the organization must be willing to accept one another before diversity can be successful. Each department, unit, team and group will determine how it will accept diverse individuals. One team may embrace diversity and be willing to work with individuals from all backgrounds. Another team may ostracize individual team members or refuse to work with other teams who have diverse members. For this reason, it is imperative to instill in the organization that all employees must work together in a cooperative manner. How can this be accomplished? The following two factors — expectations and role clarification — must be clearly spelled out between departments, units, teams and even work shifts to accomplish cooperative relationships.

Expectations

Expectations are what the organization wants and what the individual employee needs to receive from the relationship. The organization must clearly define how it expects employees to treat one another in a detailed "Code of Conduct." Appendix B provides a sample Code of Conduct. The Code of Conduct must be reviewed and signed off by all employees. The first-line supervisor should address problems, if they arise. If the first-line supervisor cannot resolve individual expectations, the complainant should have an option to file a formal grievance. This formal grievance should be reviewed by an objective leader in the organization or by an outside mediator as needed.

Role Clarification

The Code of Conduct can also help clarify the role of the individual in workplace diversity. It clarifies the individual employee's expected commitment to diversity. It also defines the expectations for all organizational members. The following is a sample statement from a Code of Conduct:

"We shall maintain a working environment that is free of harassment of any type. We are expected to show proper respect and consideration for one another at all times."

This statement clarifies the organization's expectations and identifies what role the individual must play in workplace diversity (e.g., show proper respect and consideration at all times).

Leadership Styles

There are two basic leadership styles as they relate to diversity. The open-leadership style, sometimes referred to as collaborative leadership, is committed to incorporating all individuals into the workplace. Open-style leaders have no hidden agendas and only want the organization to succeed so they quickly embrace diversity. Open-style leaders take a transformational approach to diversity; they transform the organizational culture into a collaborative working environment. A transformational leader is a trendsetter who seeks a win-win outcome for diversity and the organization.

Closed-leadership styles, or "end-of-story" managers, focus on individual achievement and success. Closed-style leaders will support diversity only if it benefits them. Figure 17 gives characteristics of closed-style leaders. ("End-Of-Story Manager," Personnel Administrator, 1989)

It obviously is *not* a good idea to have a closed-style leader coordinating the diversity efforts of the organization. In cases where this cannot be avoided, the closed-style leader must be carefully oriented about the advantages of diversity to the organization. Leadership style will ultimately make or break whether or not diversity becomes a positive force in the organization. An open-style leader must champion diversity if it is to be fully integrated into the culture. Employees respect and follow the actions of the open-style leader. The open-style leader is a positive role model for diversity because of his or her commitment and support.

FIGURE 17 Characteristics of Closed-Style Leaders

- Overly responsible
- Judge others by their belief system
- Do not allow disagreement
- Maintain status quo
- Can be prejudiced
- Mold employees
- "Bottom-line" oriented
- Rarely recognize positive contributions by the employee
- Rarely solicit input from employees
- Low tolerance for mistakes
- Inflexible
- Blame and punish

He or she views diversity as an important cultural value. On the contrary, the closed-style leader often sees diversity as a nuisance and obstruction to the success of the organization.

Assessing the Organization's Commitment

A simple assessment should be conducted to determine the level of leadership and organizational support for diversity. A representative from the human resources department, or an individual who is highly respected throughout the organization, should administer the assessment. Figure 18 provides a questionnaire that can be administered to a representative sample of employees, managers, informal leaders, senior leadership members, customers and other key stakeholders.

The responses to the questionnaire should provide very useful information about an organization and diversity. It should also help determine if the organization is committed to diversity. If possible, the organization should sample at least 25 to 50 key stakeholders to determine if any statistically valid trends can be detected. The questionnaire can be taken manually or placed on the organization's Web site. However, a large sampling could produce employee relations problems if the results are negative. Diversity has become an extremely sensitive issue for employees and society in general. The organization must be prepared to respond quickly and decisively to the assessment results.

Action Point

The organization should prepare an "Action Plan" based on the feedback from the questionnaire. The action plan should be widely communicated to employees and supervisors. The action plan should be tracked and monitored for successes and potential problems. The organization should tout successes in employee publications, at departmental meetings and on the intranet. Feedback from the questionnaire can also help identify "hot spots" in the organization that need to be addressed. For example, a low response for "Question 1" on the diversity assessment tool in Figure 18 should alert the organization to focus on the barriers that exist for individuals who are culturally diverse. After these barriers have been identified, the organization can then develop problems, policies and procedures to help address the problem areas.

Designing a Diversity Training Program

Training key stakeholders about how to effectively incorporate diversity into the culture is vital. Training helps the organization fulfill one of the significant cultural drivers identified in Figure 2. (See Introduction.)

Diversity training helps key stakeholders learn how to communicate and interact more effectively with one another. Diversity training really is "sensitivity training" because it focuses on getting in "touch with our feelings" about how to work with diverse individuals. The organization must determine if the training will be

FIGURE 18 Sample Diversity Assessment

Instructions: For each of the following statements, circle a number to indicate your estimation of the organization's support or commitment to workplace diversity.

Scale: 1 = **Strongly Disagree**
2 = **Disagree**
3 = **Neutral (Neither Agree nor Disagree)**
4 = **Agree**
5 = **Strongly Agree**

1. There are few organizational barriers present to individuals who are culturally diverse.

   1   2   3   4   5

2. The organization is committed to maintaining a workplace that treats everyone with respect and consideration.

   1   2   3   4   5

3. The organization does not practice harassment and discrimination in its employment practices.

   1   2   3   4   5

4. The organization ensures everyone has an equal opportunity to fully participate and contribute new ideas.

   1   2   3   4   5

5. The organization displays a genuine commitment to workplace diversity.

   1   2   3   4   5

6. Organizational leaders consistently display a willingness to support all employees, regardless of ethnic background, race, gender, age or other unique characteristic.

   1   2   3   4   5

7. The organization appropriately addresses any problems or barriers to diversity and equal employee access.

   1   2   3   4   5

8. The organization clearly communicates its expectations to employees regarding workplace diversity.

   1   2   3   4   5

9. Employees are well aware of their role in maintaining a diverse work environment.

   1   2   3   4   5

10. The organization actively promotes diversity as an important organizational value.

    1   2   3   4   5

conducted in house or by an outside source. In-house trainers are already known to attendees and, depending on the individual, may already possess a high level of trust. If a high trust level does exist, using in-house trainers has the advantage of gaining immediate support from program participants. If in-house trainers are used, the trainer should possess the following skills and attributes:

- **Excellent facilitator skills:** Trainers will be facilitating rather than lecturing from a static list of concepts. This means trainers will conduct "hands-on" exercises and leading group discussions instead of conducting traditional lecture-style programs.
- **Excellent communication skills:** The individual should be articulate and possess excellent listening skills. The ability to listen is important in diversity training. The facilitator will learn a great deal from participants regarding their feelings and reactions to diversity.
- **Highly credible:** Participants must see the trainer as highly trustworthy and reliable. Using individuals who are "talking heads" and not well respected will cause the training to lose credibility and support.
- **Committed to diversity:** The trainer should be highly supportive and vocal about the advantages of diversity to the organization.

Excellent in-house sources include long-term managers, opinion leaders who are widely respected in the organization, and employees who possess some of the diverse elements (e.g., ethnic background, disability, gender, race, age, etc.). The more the individual is respected and trusted, the more likely the training outcomes will be positive. If an outside training source is used, they should provide the following background information:

- **Track record:** The outside source should have a proven track record that includes experience and knowledge about workplace diversity.
- **Verifiable outcomes:** Training evaluations from other organizations should be made available to review outcomes and successes.
- **Flexibility:** The outside firm should be readily available based on the organization's timetable and needs.
- **Affordability:** The training should be affordable and comparable to what similar firms are charging.
- **Adaptability:** The training program should be adapted to the organization and not a program "off the shelf." The training must reflect the uniqueness of the organization.

The training program should help answer the following questions:

- **What is diversity?**
  - A description of the diversity factors such as age, gender, race and ethnicity
  - A discussion of the diversity elements within the organization.

- **Why is diversity important to the organization?**
  - Identify the benefits and advantages of a diverse culture.
- **Who is impacted by diversity?**
  - Discuss the positive aspects of building a diverse organization.
  - Discuss how everyone is impacted by diversity.
- **How can the individual make a difference?**
  - Discuss the importance of being open minded.
  - Identify the individual employee's role in diversity.
- **How committed is the organization to diversity?**
  - Discuss and present the organization's Code of Conduct.
  - Identify ongoing objectives of the program.

Figure 19 provides a five-module approach to diversity training. The training represents a significant time commitment by participants and trainers. It also represents a significant financial commitment by the organization. However, the outcome should be a more enlightened workforce.

Action Point

The five modules illustrated in Figure 19 represent at least 20 hours of training for every participant. An alternative to this comprehensive approach is to have an open discussion of this topic in each department/unit meeting. "Talking Points" should be provided to first-line supervisors regarding diversity. Appendix F provides sample talking points for first-line supervisors.

FIGURE 19 Sample Diversity Training Program

Module 1: Recognizing Diversity
- Program Content
- Diversity Drivers
- Elements of Diversity

Module 2: Diversity Benefits
- Benefits of a Diverse Workplace
- Enhanced Work Perspective
- Creating a Diverse Workplace

Module 3: Communication with Diverse Individuals
- Basic Communication Skills
- Skills Creating Diversity Synergy
- Role Playing

Module 4: Individual Commitment to Diversity
- Workplace Expectations
- Role Clarifications
- Power of Being Open Minded

Module 5: Ongoing Commitment
- Discussing "Code of Conduct"
- Discussing Organizational Strategy
- Identifying Team Goals

Aligning Total Rewards with Diversity

Where diversity is seen as organizational strategy and of critical value, Figure 20 provides a checklist for incorporating diversity into an organization's total rewards package.

The programs and approaches identified in Figure 20 can be customized to address an organization's wide variety of diversity needs. Paid time off (PTO), for example, often incorporates traditional vacation, holiday and sick time into one set accrual rate. Depending on the program requirements, employees can use PTO for special ethnic holidays or events without compromising or identifying their personal beliefs. It is important for organizations to continue to find new approaches to align diversity with total rewards. The best way to keep aligned is to ask for feedback from employees to determine if total rewards are meeting their unique needs. A medical organization in Kentucky created a bass fishing tournament based on feedback from employees. This tournament bridged the gap between various ethnic groups, genders, age groups, executives and employees and subgroup cultures within the organization.

For an investment of less than $1,000, this organization created a successful and fun event for its 2,300 employees. A side benefit for the organization was it became part of the organization's culture. It was an event that employees continue to enjoy and talk about around the water cooler.

FIGURE 20 Checklist of Total Rewards Programs and Approaches that Address Diversity

☐ Career development program	☐ Legal insurance
☐ Career ladder	☐ Long-term care coverage
☐ Continuing education program	☐ On-site child care
☐ Corporate university	☐ On-site convenience services
☐ Culture diversity days aimed at sharing ethnic information	☐ Paid time off
☐ Domestic partners program	☐ Scholarship programs for children of employees
☐ Employee assistance program	☐ Service awards
☐ Employee health program	☐ Smoking cessation programs
☐ Extended leave program, which provides time off beyond FMLA requirements	☐ Spot recognition
	☐ Succession planning
	☐ Telecommuting
☐ Financial counseling	☐ Transfer and promotion opportunity programs
☐ Fitness and wellness programs	
☐ Flexible staffing	☐ Tuition reimbursement
☐ Job sharing	

To obtain input from employees about diversity, the use of "issue-oriented" surveys can be very effective. The "issue-oriented" survey focuses on two to three questions about various aspects of total rewards. These surveys can focus on how to incorporate diversity into the total rewards programs. The following are some examples of potential questions:

1. Does the organization do a good job of providing total rewards programs that meet the unique needs of all its employees?

    ____Yes   ____No

    If no, please tell us what we could offer or change in our existing programs:

    _____
    _____
    _____

    _____

2. Does the organization provide training opportunities to all employees regardless of race, gender, disability or national origin?

    ____Yes   ____No

    If no, how should the organization address this issue? Please elaborate:

    _____
    _____
    _____
    _____

    _____

3. Do you believe the organization provides equal opportunities for all employees regarding promotional and job-growth opportunities?

    ____Yes   ____No

    If you answered no, please identify some ways we could improve in this area:

    _____
    _____
    _____
    _____

    _____

Issue-oriented surveys are easy to administer. They can be used as payroll stuffers or placed on the organization's intranet or Web site. The bottom line is to look for various ways to keep total rewards programs in tune with diversity. The issue-oriented survey and other feedback mechanisms will provide leadership with useful data to make this happen.

Discussion Point

One caution is that an issue-oriented survey can raise concerns if feedback to employees is not provided. The organization must be prepared to show employees how they responded and how they used their input to make constructive changes to total rewards programs.

An action plan is provided in Chapter 5, Figure 31. It incorporates some of the concepts and tools discussed in this chapter. Next, an organization's cultural profile will determine the support level for diversity.

Developing Cultural Goals 3

Culture helps define and control behavior within the organization. Examples of behavior controlled by the culture include:

- Innovation versus Status Quo: The degree to which organizational members are allowed to be innovative and creative is determined by the organizational culture. Innovation is one of the behaviors encouraged by strong cultures. (See Figure 7.)
- Individual versus Team Orientation: The degree to which the culture builds work activities around an individual or team approach.
- Process versus Goals and Outcomes: Does the organization focus on processes and work methods or the achievement of goals and measurable outcomes?
- Centralized versus Decentralized Decision Making: How much involvement does the employee have in the decision-making process? A centralized culture relies on the approval from the top before implementing new ideas and valuable changes.
- Cooperative versus Competitive: Does the culture encourage employees to be cooperative and exhibit a team spirit or is individual competition valued and rewarded?

These are just examples of how culture impacts the organization. Culture can be a liability or asset to the organization's strategic direction. For example, weak cultures built around the individual and the status quo actually create a barrier to change and improvement. However, a culture that focuses on team spirit and innovation makes it easier to try new strategies and to grow the business so organizations should build a cultural profile.

Designing a Cultural Profile

A starting point for creating a profile is to look at what other successful organizations have done. Figure 21 offers insight into how some of the organizations listed in *Fortune's* "100 Top Companies to Work For" incorporated culture into their operations.

These employee-friendly organizations have enriched cultures that value people and diversity. The 10 common threads in Figure 21 comprise an impressive cultural profile. Not all organizations have, or want, all 10 of these elements. In fact, some organizations may be more focused on No. 4 in Figure 21 (i.e., "financially secure") rather than valuing people or diversity. The bottom line is to design a cultural profile of what most closely represents the organization and its strategic direction. The following five questions will help in the designing a profile:

1. **WHAT does the organization value most?**

    The answer to this question is not as simple as it may first appear. For example, the organization may value their employees but for survival must also place a high value on revenue and lower costs. Another organization may place a high value on customers. In this case, the cultural profile will be centered on the organization's customers. This cultural profile may include developing superior customer relations skills and valuing individuals who can relate to the customer. Two examples of organizations that place a high value on customer relations include The Ritz-Carlton and the Four Seasons Hotel. They hire for "attitude" and build their cultural profile around service delivery.

2. **HOW does the organization want to look?**

    This question refers to the mental image the company wants to create with customers and key stakeholders. The organization may want to be seen as a "socially conscious" entity committed to the community and to less fortunate individuals. A cultural profile under those circumstances will focus on people and social causes. Ken Blanchard, a best-selling business author, is the chief spiritual officer of Kenneth Blanchard Companies, which provides a unique perk to its employees. They are given a lump sum each year to donate to a social cause of their choice. The excitement this perk has generated is immeasurable and, as a result, employees and outsiders see Kenneth Blanchard Companies as a caring and compassionate organization. The retail clothing store Hot Topic, on the other hand, wants to be seen as a fun place to work. This image helps recruit young people to work for it and creates a connection with its younger customer base. To project this image, Hot Topic's CEO puts orange streaks in her hair and employees are free to dress like rock stars.

3. **WHO is responsible for guiding the organization's success?**

    For some organizations, the CEO is primarily responsible for guiding the organization. Jack Welch, General Electric's former CEO, crafted a culture that

FIGURE 21 Cultural Profile of Organizations Listed in the '100 Best Companies to Work For'

1. **A Commitment to Development and Learning**
    - Unique tuition reimbursements and scholarships offered
    - Corporate universities established on site for employee convenience
    - Promotions opportunities provided to individuals who increase their personal knowledge.
2. **Unique People Practices**
    - "Nerd lunches" and other novel approaches
    - Decentralized decision making so employees are empowered to participate
    - No layoff policies, even in poor financial times.
3. **Supportive Leadership**
    - A family-style leader who is committed to the success of the organization and its people
    - Servant leadership that puts the employee first
    - Innovative leaders who were not afraid to try new and better ways of doing things.
4. **Financially Secure**
    - Organizations are consistently profitable.
    - Average salaries are on the high end for their industry.
    - Job growth and employment are healthy and steady.
5. **Health and Well-Being Are Encouraged**
    - Fitness and health are encouraged by the organization (e.g., on-site fitness centers.)
6. **Employees are Recognized and Rewarded for Contributions**
    - Employee recognition is practiced and valued.
    - Unique recognition programs such as weekend retreats are offered.
    - Leaders are trained about how to effectively recognize and reward employees.
7. **Work-Life Balancing is Supported by the Organization**
    - Flexible work schedules are offered.
    - Part-time employees are provided attractive benefits.
    - Telecommuting and other innovative work-life practices are offered.
8. **Work Environments are Positive and Attractive**
    - Family-oriented work environments that value the employee.
    - Flexible policies and procedures that seek to create an open work environment.
    - Attractive and well-kept physical facilities are the general norm.
    - Employees are provided with appropriate supplies and equipment to do the job.
9. **Diversity is Valued by the Organization**
    - The organizations provide equal opportunity to all individuals.
    - The workplace is representative of the area the organization seeks to serve.
    - Unique diversity approaches, such as Cultural Awareness Days, are provided.
10. **Organization Structure Encourages Employee Input**
    - Team participation is encouraged and valued.
    - Organizational leaders are highly visible to employees.
    - The organization has innovative methods for the employee to provide feedback on change and other issues.

was "mean and lean." GE's cultural profile valued creativity while keeping costs low and revenues high. Leadership is generally the key element in designing a cultural profile. Employees look to leadership to help define the culture. However, some cultures are more employee driven. Monsanto uses "people teams" to develop bonding activities. The board of directors guides other organizations, like many large investment banking firms. Board-directed organizations are going to be more driven by profit, productivity and cost containment. The key is to know of the organization's chief architects, who must have prominent roles in designing the cultural profile. In reality, those individuals have already shaped the culture in some way. The goal is to use these individuals as "champions" to make positive cultural changes as necessary.

4. **WHERE does the organization want to go?**

   The answer to this question may be in the organization's strategic plan. Some organizations have well-defined "futures." To reach this "future" state, the organization probably will need to redesign its cultural profile. In cases where the strategic plan does not clearly define the organization's direction, key leaders may need to conduct an internal analysis that looks at the strengths and weaknesses of the organization. After identifying *strengths and weaknesses*, the organization will then need to complete an external analysis to determine *opportunities and threats*. This simple *SWOT analysis* helps the organization to determine its strategic direction. It also paints an accurate picture of the current state of the organization. From this picture, an accurate cultural profile can be created that focuses on strengths and opportunities.

5. **HOW accurate is the organization's mission and vision in describing "who we are"?**

   This question should be the first one addressed because it may be necessary to revisit what is truly important to the organization. The mission and vision is so important to the cultural profile that it must be absolutely accurate. Some mission statements really fail in defining "who we are." The same can be said for vision statements because they sometimes fail to state accurately "where we want to go." Mission and vision statements may need to be redefined before designing the cultural profile. This is necessary because the goal of the cultural profile is to define "who we are" *and* "what we hope to become."

The senior leadership team, with input from key stakeholders, should carefully answer the above questions about its culture. Once these questions are answered, the organization is ready to craft its cultural profile, expectations and strategic direction.

Figure 22 depicts a hypothetical organization's cultural profile and its answers to the five key questions. Compare the example in Figure 22 to some of the 10 key elements in Figure 21 that some of the "100 Best Companies" said were important.

FIGURE 22 **Magna Corp.**

Cultural Profile

1. HOW accurate is the organization's mission and vision?
   Answer: Organization no longer focuses on a worldwide market. This changes where we want to go and who we are.
2. WHAT does the organization value most?
   Answer: Our loyal customer base.
3. HOW does the organization want to look?
   Answer: We want to be seen as a regionally based firm committed to its customers and employees. All employees are equally valued.
4. WHO is responsible for guiding the organization?
   Answer: The senior leadership team comprised of the CEO and six divisional vice presidents.
5. WHERE does the organization want to go?
   Answer: To become a major provider of fitness equipment for the Midwest market.

Resulting Cultural Profile

1. Customer Focused
   - Customer training is provided to all employees.
   - Organization focuses on customer preferences and changing needs.
2. Employees are Valued by the Organization
   - Unique employee benefits programs are provided.
   - Flexible work schedules are offered.
   - Employee recognition is readily encouraged.
3. Fitness and Well-Being is Encouraged
   - In keeping with the organization's strategy, employee wellness is encouraged and nurtured.
   - On-site fitness centers equipped with the organization's products are in place.
   - Wellness is recognized organizationwide on a monthly, quarterly and annual basis.
4. Diversity is Valued and Supported By Leadership
   - The senior leadership team is committed to a diverse working environment.
   - The organization provides equal access to all employees and job applicants.
   - The composition of the workforce is representative of the Midwest regional area.
5. Organizational Growth is Highly Valued
   - The organization seeks new ways to expand market potential.
   - Employee ideas are encouraged and valued.
   - The senior leadership team is highly visible with the staff.

Magna Corp. in Figure 22 has developed a profile that reflects what it would like to achieve. Obviously, the cultural profile is more than just painting a random picture. The profile is truly the organization's identity and helps guide the strategic direction. The organization must continually revisit the profile and tweak it as changes are made. No organization is completely static. The same is true for the cultural profile. The profile should accurately reflect the current organization and not "what used to be." Keeping the profile current is a challenge for leaders and all key stakeholders. In Chapter 7, the authors will discuss the value of conducting annual cultural surveys, which help keep the profile current and fresh.

Discussion Point

Is the cultural profile an accurate reflection of the culture? In a shared culture, key stakeholders generally have an opportunity to review and common about the validity of the profile. In a closed culture, the CEO or an outside consulting firm may develop the profile. In this case, the profile may be more the "ideal" than the actual culture. There are a good number of closed cultures that do not involve employees or other key stakeholders in developing the profile. In this case, the profile may represent more of a marketing or public relations tool than an actual resource for accurately depicting the culture. The cultural profile should describe what the organization values and seeks to embrace. A profile is not meant to be an ideal marketing tool. It should include the "warts and wrinkles" of the organization. The reality is most organizations have many problems contained within their culture. The profile should not seek to make value judgments about the culture but instead be indicative of what organization truly values. In some cases, these values are established by leaders and owners of the organization. It remains the employees' decision of how they can embrace or even remain a part of the identified profile.

Measuring the Effectiveness of the Culture

Three important measurement tools can be used to help assess the effectiveness of culture to the organization: cultural goals, the culture scorecard and leadership assessment.

Cultural goals generally reflect the cultural profile developed from the five questions discussed previously. Magna Corp., the hypothetical organization in Figure 22, focused on customer service. A cultural goal regarding customer service follows, along with measurement elements:

Customer service: *To provide customer service training to all employees*

Measurement elements

- Increase customer satisfaction by 10 percent.
- Reduce customer complaints by 20 percent.
- Employees score at least 90 percent on customer service training assessment.

Magna Corp. can track the success of the customer training by comparing employee performance with stated objectives. Another example of how to track cultural goals is illustrated in Appendix A. One of the strategic goals of the template for cultural diversity was to "increase employees awareness of workplace diversity." Increased awareness could be measured by tracking job satisfaction rates on the employee opinion survey or by simply doing periodic "issue-oriented" surveys focused on employee awareness. Developing measurable goals is a key to measuring cultural effectiveness. The results of each tool can be widely communicated to key stakeholders via the culture scorecard.

The **culture scorecard** is the definitive tool for measuring and communicating the effectiveness of culture. It details how the organization is performing relative to its cultural profile. The scorecard is unique because the cultural profile is different for all organizations. Figure 23 provides a sample culture scorecard based on the five elements identified in Figure 22 for Magna Corp.

Based on the scorecard, Magna Corp. needs to work diligently on customer service, cultural diversity and employee wellness. The culture scorecard tells organizations how "they are doing" in maintaining and growing the culture. Some of the information gathered in the annual cultural survey can be used to supplement and provide data to the culture scorecard. (See Appendix D.)

Discussion Point

The cultural survey can identify problem areas, such as cultural diversity issues, that should be monitored and tracked by the scorecard. The scorecard can be used to communicate to key stakeholders the importance of culture to the organization. The following guidelines help the scorecard to be seen as an effective tool and a credible and objective resource:

- The scorecard should be shared with a wide audience including employees, managers and board members.
- Negative results should be discussed and an action plan formulated about how to address areas of concern.
- The scorecard should be communicated on a consistent and timely basis.
- The format of the scorecard should be easy to follow and understand.
- The scorecard does not overstate or understate the impact of culture on the organization.
- The scorecard data is accurate and complete.
- Leaders use the scorecard as a resource.

A **leadership assessment** should be conducted at least annually regarding the influence of culture on the organization. The leadership assessment should be brief and address five key areas:

- The leader's comfort level with the cultural profile
- How much the leader values culture and diversity as important to the organization's success

FIGURE 23 Sample Scorecard

Quarter/Month: Test Month/Quarter, (Year)

Customer Service

Measure	Target	Actual	Variance	YTD Variance
1. Percent of favorable response on customer surveys	90%	75%	-15%	-15%
2. Customer compliments received	50	46	-4	-12

Employee Morale

Measure	Target	Actual	Variance	YTD Variance
1. Job satisfaction based on quarterly surveys or annual cultural assessment	85%	90%	+5%	+5%
2. Employee turnover (Quarterly)	3%	2%	+1%	+1%
3. Morale indicator based on a composite of job satisfaction and cultural acceptance measures on issue-oriented surveys	90%	92%	+2%	+2%
4. Job vacancy rate	12%	8%	+4%	+4%

Employee Wellness

Measure	Target	Actual	Variance	YTD Variance
1. Percent of employee participation in the organization's fitness center	40%	30%	-10%	-10%
2. Number of employees recognized for their commitment to wellness (monthly)	100	71	-29	-29
3. Percent reduction in health insurance usage by employees	15%	8%	-7%	-7%

FIGURE 23 **Sample Scorecard** *(Continued)*

Quarter/Month: Test Month/Quarter, (Year)

Cultural Diversity

Measure	Target	Actual	Variance	YTD Variance
1. Percent of employees completing diversity training	100%	95%	-5	-5%
2. Turnover of culturally diverse employees.	5%	9%	+4%	+4%
3. Harassment claims	0	2	-2	-2
4. Percent of culturally diverse employees in leadership roles	25%	15%	-10%	-10%

Organizational Growth

Measure	Target	Actual	Variance	YTD Variance
1. Number of employee suggestions	50	61	+11	+11
2. Increase in productivity	10%	12%	+2%	+2%
3. Number of rounds by executive leadership team to employee's work area	30	42	+12	+12

- How well the leader understands and can articulate the importance of culture and diversity
- The leader's assessment of how the employee views culture and diversity
- How committed the leader believes the organization is to the value of culture and diversity.

As the cultural profile changes over time, the leader assessment needs to be revised to gather pertinent information. As changes occur, leaders should be encouraged to discuss their thoughts and beliefs regarding culture and diversity. This type of feedback is critical to understanding cultural impact and developing ongoing cultural strategy. The assessment tool should be administered by a highly credible and trustworthy source. The results of the assessment should be communicated to leaders in group meetings. A simple written summary could be sent from the chief executive officer to all organizational leaders. A sample leadership assessment is shown in Figure 24.

 **Action Point**
The leadership assessment should be conducted after the cultural profile has been developed. This allows organizational leaders to comment on the impact of culture on the work experience and the validity of the cultural profile. Not surprising, this assessment often uncovers a disconnect between what top leadership thinks the profile should be and what the first-line leaders actually experience daily. It is obviously up to top leadership if this disconnect should be embraced and used as an opportunity to "self-correct" a potentially inaccurate profile.

Aligning Organizational Strategy with Cultural Goals

The Magna Corp. example in Figure 22 provided a glimpse of how organizational strategy can be aligned with cultural goals. One of the elements of the cultural profile for Magna Corp. was: "organizational growth is highly valued." The cultural profile provides an excellent starting point for organizations to build their strategy. To have a successful strategy, the organization must have the capability to achieve its goals. The cultural profile defines "who we are" and "what we value." From the profile, culture goals can be developed similar to the "customer service goal" developed as a measure of cultural effectiveness. Culture goals should be an integral resource in building the organization's strategy. Figure 25 illustrates this simple three-step process in aligning goals.

- Step 1: Develop a cultural profile of the organization.
- Step 2: Use the profile to develop cultural imperatives for the organization.
- Step 3: Integrate the cultural goals and profile into the organization's strategic objectives.

Figure 25 focused on organizational growth and how to align culture with strategic objectives. This example may need to be tweaked as the other parts of the cultural profile are integrated into the strategy. When the organization is finished with this process, it will have a strategic plan that is aligned with the culture. The key to this alignment process is to develop good cultural goals and imperatives. Cultural imperatives are aspects of the culture that must be incorporated into the overall strategy. For example, if an organization is to grow, it must rely on the creativity and knowledge of its employees. The development of cross-functional teams is important to the organization's growth and ability to compete. This assessment process should continue with all of the cultural imperatives until an integrated strategy is crafted.

At this point, cultural goals, imperatives and strategies have been developed. The next chapter links culture with the working environment.

FIGURE 24 Sample Leadership Assessment

Instructions: We need to know your assessment of the effect of culture on the organization. For each of the following statements, indicate your level of agreement based on the scale below:

Scale: 1 = **Strongly Disagree**

2 = **Disagree**

3 = **Neutral (Neither Agree or Disagree)**

4 = **Agree**

5 = **Strongly Agree**

1. I am comfortable with how culture and diversity have been integrated into the organization.

   1   2   3   4   5

2. I personally value organizational culture as an important aspect of work-life.

   1   2   3   4   5

3. I fully understand the components of the organization's culture.

   1   2   3   4   5

4. I am committed to creating and maintaining a diverse culture built on trust and equality.

   1   2   3   4   5

5. Employees believe culture is an important aspect of their work experience.

   1   2   3   4   5

6. The organization is committed to understanding, and developing as possible, the impact of culture and diversity on the employee's work experience.

   1   2   3   4   5

7. How would you describe the organization's cultural profile? Please elaborate below:
   _____
   _____
   _____

8. What can the organization do to enhance its culture? Please elaborate below:
   _____
   _____
   _____

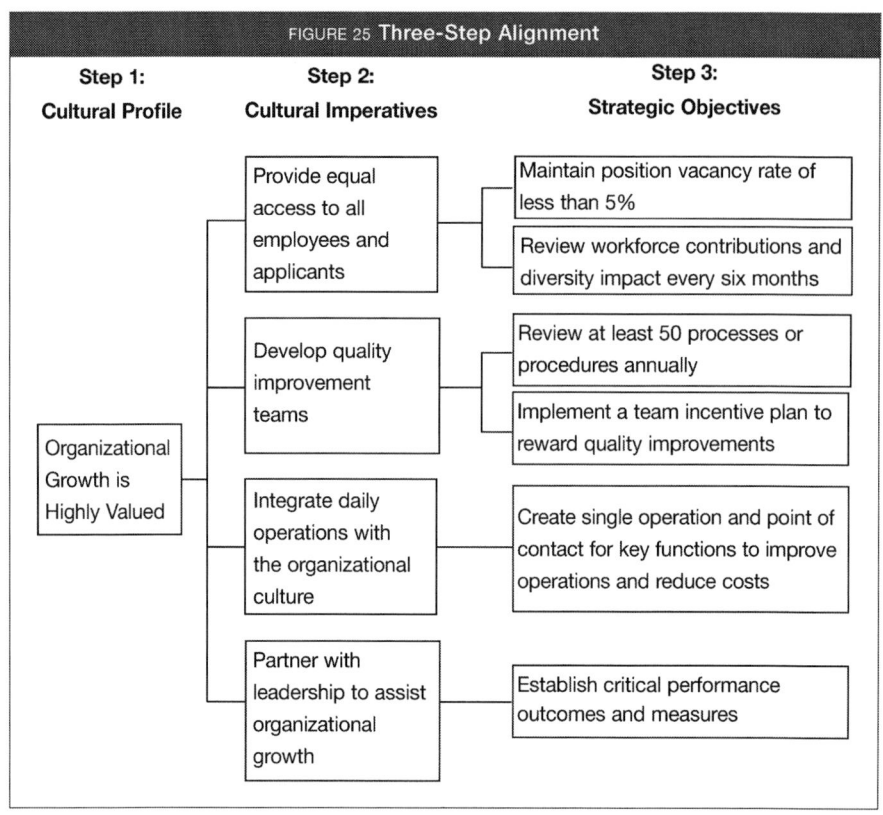

FIGURE 25 **Three-Step Alignment**

Environment Versus Culture — Defining Environment 4

Ever hear someone say after he/she is hired into an organization: "This place sure is different than what I thought it would be?" The reason could be that the workplace environment is generally different than the culture. Environment is shaped by clear definitions of jobs, the workplace and the company. Figure 26 shows some components of a working environment. Notice all of these components are clearly defined elements in the workplace.

The environment is the formal part of the organization. It defines the "daily operations" by providing formal structure and definitions. For example, job design clearly determines how individual employees perform their work. The job content can be totally defined for employees or based loosely on how the job has been performed historically.

FIGURE 26 Components of a Working Environment

Job Design
- Level of independent decision making by the person in the job
- Job content
- How the job interacts with other positions in the organization
- Physical and mental requirements for the job
- Job specifications
- Availability of equipment and supplies
- Work schedule.

Organizational Climate
- Job satisfaction level of the employee
- Overall organizational morale.

Decision Making
- Centralized versus decentralized decision making
- Employee involvement in decision making
- Team decision making.

Policies and Procedures
- Formal, written guidelines for various aspects of the organization
- Flexible versus structured policies and procedures.

Physical Plant
- Layout of the organization
- Building design
- Geographic location
- Safety and security elements of the physical plant.

The Company
- Company's reputation and public relations image
- Public perception of the organization
- Company's identity and success stories
- Visible leaders
- Mission and vision.

Organizational climate determines how employees feel about the formal workplace. Organizational climate and culture are two different concepts. When employees say morale is low, they are generally referring to their dissatisfaction with the formal organization. This could be dissatisfaction with a policy, procedure, lack of equipment, schedule, safety aspects or some other element in the organization's formal structure. Formal policy, organizational structure or leadership often determines how the organization makes decisions. The home office, department or work site can make decisions. This determines if decision making is centralized or decentralized. Again, formal structure generally determines this. Policies and procedures can be well defined and very structured, which will make for a very controlled work environment. They also can be loose and too flexible, which can result in an out-of-control environment ruled by the "squeaky wheel." In this case, the employee who yells the loudest determines the policy for that day. This type of environment leads to anarchy and discord.

Discussion Point

Some managers may equate climate with culture. It is what managers often refer to when they think and respond to cultural concerns. Culture is more extensive than the environment's overall morale or the organizational climate. Culture is an organizational driver for many facets of the organization, including the development of total rewards programs. It is a mistake to focus on climate as the sole cultural component. At any time, climate may change direction depending on what is going on in the organization. For example, the lowering of health-insurance premiums certainly would impact the organizational climate. However, this event would not change the organization's culture. Cultural change is a more long-term and less dependent on policy changes or events.

The physical plant plays a unique role in defining environment. The layout of the organization can be pleasant and readily accessible. Many of us have been in organizations that are disorganized, with physical facilities that are in disrepair. What about the location? The physical plant cannot be moved or relocated very easily. This is when total rewards programs come into play. Telecommuting and relocation assistance are examples of how to help employees cope with an undesirable location.

Safety and security are important factors in the working environment. Most organizations monitor safety and have in-house safety committees to address problems. Unsafe work practices must be identified and changed immediately to safeguard the employee and the organization's reputation. Organizations are becoming more aware of security as workplace violence becomes a major concern for employees. According to the National Institute for Occupational Safety and Health, workplace violence was the leading cause of death in the workplace for females in 2003 and 2004 and the second leading cause of death in the workplace for males. This sobering statistic indicates the importance of having a secure and safe working environment.

Finally, the company sets the tone for the environment. Companies with good reputations in the community make it easier to attract and retain committed employees. A poor public image can detract from the work experience and make it virtually impossible to build a positive environment.

Comparing Culture and Environment

Culture is the "unwritten values" of an organization whereas the environment is defined by the formal structure and policies of the organization. Culture and environment often overlap one another. Figure 27 compares the cultural components that were originally identified in Figure 3 to the components of a working environment detailed in Figure 26. The components of both provide an unusual comparison. For example, espoused values are often encompassed into the organizational climate and the policies and procedures components of environment. Espoused values are formal values that are written and publicly communicated. When the organization deviates from its espoused values, organizational morale can be dramatically impacted. This is just one example of how culture and environment overlap and impact one another.

Organizational norms should be integrated into a company's policies and procedures. For example, if an organizational norm is to have perfect attendance, then the organization should have a corresponding attendance policy that defines what the it expects.

FIGURE 27 **Comparing Culture to Environment**

Cultural Component	Environmental Component(s)
• Values	• Organizational Climate/ Policies and Procedures
• Norms	• Policies and Procedures
• Leadership	• The Company
• Patterns of Behavior	• Organizational Climate
• Communication Style	• Decision Making
• Beliefs and Rituals	• The Company/Policies and Procedures
• Mission	• The Company
• Cultural Sensitivity	• Job Design/Organizational Climate/The Company
Cultural Component	**Environmental Component(s)**
• Diversity	• Policies and Procedures/ Job Design/The Company
• Formality	• Policies and Procedures/ Physical Plant
• Innovation	• Decision Making/Job Design
• Trust	• Organizational Climate/ The Company

The attendance policy reinforces the organizational norm and provides a structure from which to make it work. Group norms are part of the unwritten culture. They are rarely defined except in organizations having self-directed work teams.

Leadership is a cultural component that overlaps many of the environmental elements. However, the most favorable comparison of leadership with environment is "the company" component. Leaders must be visible with their key stakeholders to build the reputation and image of the organization. This is how employees and other key stakeholders develop their perception about the organization. I worked with a leader who rarely met with employees and, in fact, avoided contact with the organization's customers. The organization soon became known as a "standoffish" place in which to work and do business. Ultimately, it had to remove him from his leadership role. Group and individual patterns of behavior surface in the organizational climate. How employees treat and interact with one another is clearly evident in the overall organizational morale.

The decision-making process best shows an organization's communication style. Centralized decision making results in a closed style of communication in which decisions are made from the top down. Open communication style is most evident in environments that have decentralized decision making and encourage employee involvement.

The defined beliefs and rituals of a culture are most often contained in the company's image and within its policies and procedures. If employees are highly valued, policies and procedures may be more flexible and "user friendly." The espoused mission should be interwoven in the company's reputation, impact and public persona. Because the mission is "who we are," it should reflect how others see the organization.

Cultural sensitivity resonates with job design, organizational climate and the company. The goal of cultural sensitivity should be a high level of awareness of all individuals. It is impacted by how we design jobs, how we treat and interact with one another in the organization's climate, and the overall propensity for the company to accept cultural differences. Diversity overlaps with job design and the company's reputation for the same reasons as cultural sensitivity. It also overlaps with policies and procedures that must be in place to ensure there is a diverse workplace.

Formality is generally well defined by the organization's policies and procedures. For example, the structure of an organization's policies regarding attendance, performance and discipline may indicate a more formal work environment. Physical plant and the layout of the work areas are indicative of how formal or informal an organization wants to be perceived. Hot Topic, for example, wants to be seen as an informal workplace built on fun and youthful energy. General Electric's physical plants are generally well organized and very formal.

Innovation is a cultural component that is either encouraged or discouraged. Decentralized decision making and a flexible job design are indicative of an environment that supports an innovative culture.

Finally, trust is a cultural component that is clearly evident in the organization's climate and the company's overall perception. When there is a low level of trust by the employees, the organizational climate will generally be negative. The organization's overall image will suffer when trust becomes an issue. Enron is an example of where a low level of trust ultimately destroyed the company's reputation and image with its employees and customers.

Linking Culture with Environment

The first step to linking culture with environment is to determine which elements of each favorably compare. Figure 27 helped accomplish this task. Step 2 is actually linking culture and environment. This means linking the formal structure, represented by the environment, with the identified cultural goals and profile of the organization. The "Code of Conduct" detailed in Appendix B provides an example of how to absorb cultural values and diversity into the organization. Elements of the environment should also be included in the "Code of Conduct" and the "Cultural Strategic Plan." (See Appendix A.) Figure 28 offers an example of how the environmental elements of health and safety could be included in the "Code of Conduct." Each element of the environment could be addressed in the "Code of Conduct" depending on how the organization wants to frame the formal structure. It is important that environmental elements play a significant role in the organization's cultural strategy.

FIGURE 28 **How to Insert Environmental Elements into the Code of Conduct**

Environmental Considerations

- We shall maintain a drug-free, smoke-restricted environment. Smoking is permitted only in specifically designated areas.
- We shall report any practice or condition that may violate any rule, regulation or safety standard to the appropriate supervisor or department.
- We will report all unusual events or accidents, by both verbal and written report, involving a customer, an employee or a vendor in a timely manner.
- We will be alerted to equipment failures and report any hazards or malfunctions to supervisors.
- We recognize that possession of a deadly weapon while on duty or on the premises is strictly forbidden.
- We will strive to protect employees, customers and the environment from exposure to hazardous materials and toxic fumes.

The tone expressed in Figure 28 is one of regulation and structure. It is expressed to reinforce the organization's formal efforts at maintaining a healthy and safe culture. In this manner, the formal organization is establishing guidelines and controls for ensuring a healthy and safe environment. Guidelines and controls are two important elements for effectively linking culture with environment.

Discussion Point

It is important to note that a "Code of Conduct" must be very formal and structured. This may appear to be an "all or nothing" approach to leadership. In some regard, this reflects a "Theory X" or "top-down" approach to communicating the environment. When establishing basic guidelines for the environment, it is important that employees clearly understand what the organization values. The "Code of Conduct" provides a comprehensive guide to how top leadership wants the formal organization to function. It is a basic and simplistic approach to establishing rules of order. How the code is communicated and enacted may be more representative of the individual manager's style. This can be problematic if leadership style prevents a consistent interpretation of the code's basic intent. In reality, this is what sometimes occurs as individual management styles impact the ultimate intent of this code.

Below is an example of how the formal environment links education with the diversity strategic plan.

Cultural Diversity Goal: To provide education to all employees about the importance of diversity to the organization.

Environment Component(s):
- All employees must attend diversity training at least annually in accordance with performance policy and procedure.
- The vision of the organization is that all employees are treated with dignity and respect.
- Work schedules will be adjusted to accommodate diversity training.
- A schedule of diversity training classes will also be offered to the public.

In the example, environment components support and mandate diversity training. Notice that the organization also seeks to enhance its image by offering diversity classes to the public. If the organization is not really providing a diverse environment to its employees, this feeble attempt at offering diversity classes to the public could backfire. It is important that the organization ensure that the cultural and environmental elements are in tandem.

Step 3 is to create a roadmap of where the organization wants the culture and environment to meet. This is an ambitious process because it involves creating a "future state" of the organization. This may need to be changed if the organization's environment cannot fully absorb its cultural needs. Figure 29 provides a busy roadmap that looks at all processes and programs that will integrate culture with the environment. Note this is only an example because the roadmap is different for all organizations. The roadmap must try to capture the unique qualities of the organization's culture and environment. Also note that the organization in this case has chosen to implement a new spot recognition program and develop workplace teams. These two environmental elements have been implemented to support the cultural components identified in the roadmap. The last stop before arriving at the "final destination" is to integrate cultural goals with the company's strategic plan. This is a critical piece on the roadmap because it is the final action necessary to integrate culture with the environment.

Step 4 involves conducting an internal analysis to determine the common strengths and weaknesses present in the culture and the environment. Figure 30 provides a sample internal analysis that looks at strengths and weaknesses. This example is only a partial analysis as many other strengths and weaknesses could probably be identified. A review of the strengths illustrates how culture and environment reinforce one another. For example, this organization has already developed its cultural profile. To support this cultural initiative, the environment has put in place supportive policies, procedures and workplace practices. A review of the weaknesses

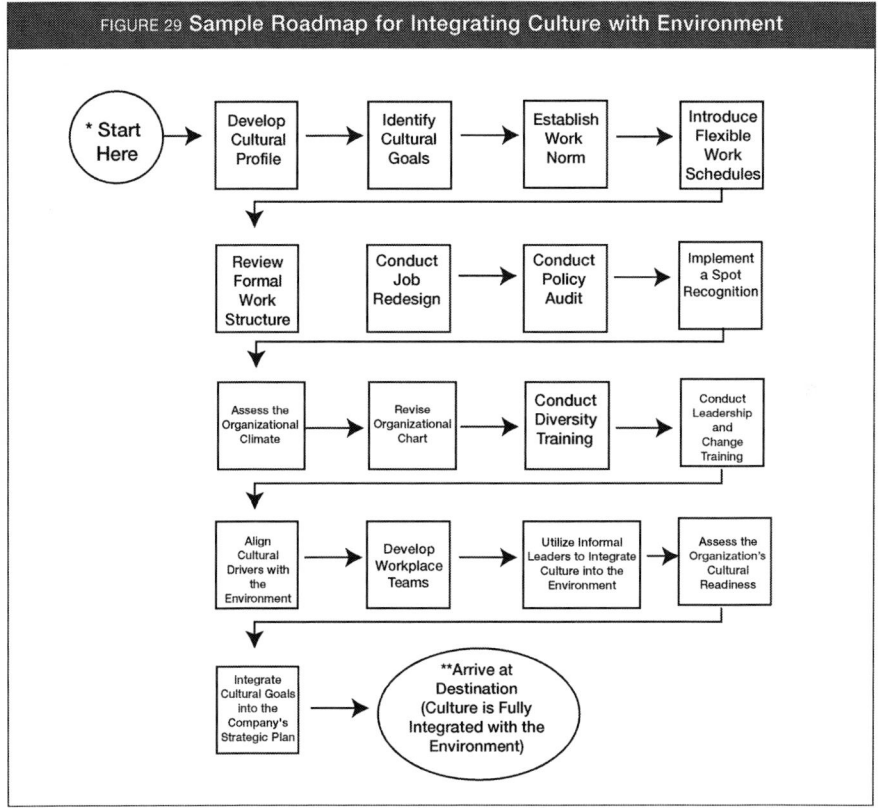

FIGURE 29 Sample Roadmap for Integrating Culture with Environment

FIGURE 30 Sample Internal Analysis

Common Strengths	Common Weaknesses
Culture • Cultural profile has been developed • Cultural goals have been identified **Environment** • Supportive policies, procedures and practices in place • Company has excellent community image	**Culture** • Cultural success stores not readily shared • Cultural diversity not widely supported • Organizational climate is currently ill-prepared and morale is low **Environment** • Physical layout is not conducive to individuals with disabilities

results in the same culture and environment linkage. The culture has not readily shared its successes, such as implementing work-life strategies. The organizational climate is ill prepared and morale is low because employees and key stakeholders have not been kept informed. When an organization fails to share its successes, it creates a "self-fulfilling prophecy" that it does not care for its employees. This self-fulfilling prophecy will take time to overcome.

The fifth and final step is to create an action plan that addresses the cultural and environmental weaknesses. There are four key areas in the action plan:

1. **Action(s):** This area of the action plan details what the organization plans to do to address identified weaknesses.
2. **Resources:** This area details the human and financial resources that are needed to address each action step.
3. **Outcomes:** The expected outcomes of implementing each action step.
4. **Timetable:** The identified timelines needed to address each action step.

Figure 31 is a sample action plan based on cultural diversity, which was one of the four weaknesses identified in Figure 30. The plan takes a simplistic approach to addressing how to gain support for cultural diversity. If an action plan is too elaborate, it will cause leaders and other key stakeholders to disregard it. A complex action plan for a "soft area" like culture or environment has a tendency to turn off senior leadership. The action plan should be easy to understand and communicate to all key stakeholders.

Note that the plan in Figure 31 has added a new player to help with developing and communicating cultural diversity within the organization. This new player is the diversity coordinator, who should be highly credible and trusted within the organization. The coordinator's chief role is to give structure within the environment regarding diversity. The communication plan in the ninth action step should be structure but easily understood by all key stakeholders. We will revisit the communication plan in Chapter 7.

Finally, the emergence of a valuable resource is evident in the action plan. The executive champion provides support to all important cultural and work-life strategies. The executive champion is a member of the senior leadership team who actively supports and understands the importance of positive cultural and environmental change. It is virtually impossible to develop a diverse culture without support from top leadership. The executive champion does not have to be the CEO but must occupy a position of respect and power. An executive champion should be identified early in the process to legitimize the change efforts. Once this individual is on board and committed, the rest of the organization is likely to follow.

Developing Environment-Friendly Total Rewards Programs

Some interesting total rewards programs have already been identified in Chapter 2. (See Figure 20.) These programs promoted diversity and cultural change. To align these programs with the environment, it is important to provide structure and support for these work-life strategies. Work-life strategies are those programs and approaches that promote cultural goals, diversity and equal workplace access. The environmental element is to take these strategies and develop formal programs and policies to support them. The environment provides the infrastructure for these cultural changes to happen. For example, a telecommuting program involves the following key environmental elements:

- **Guidelines and controls:** The program must have formal guidelines about what is expected. Controls ensure the program will be monitored and adjusted if needed.
- **Organizational support:** The program must have the support of leadership, employees and other key stakeholders. It should not be seen as the program "du jour," which would be a short-term "fix" to provide work-life effectiveness.
- **Appropriate rewards:** The program should offer attractive and appropriate rewards to the employee participants. The organization is still responsible for paying competitive wages and offering other total rewards programs that will attract rather than detract from offering it as a work-life strategy.
- **Flexibility:** The program should have some built-in flexibility that allows participants to really balance work and life. A telecommuting program that only exists on certain days of the week, fixed shifts or blocks of time hardly provides much work-life balance.
- **Interaction:** For the program to be successful, participants must still be able to interact with the formal organization. The employee must still be able to provide valuable input about their work life and offer suggestions for improving the

FIGURE 31 Sample Action Plan for Cultural Diversity

Action(s)	Resources	Expected Outcome(s)	Timetable
1. Conduct a diversity assessment with all key stakeholders.	• Senior Leadership Team • Human Resources Representative • Employees • Managers • Outside consultants as needed.	Determine level of leadership and organizational support for diversity.	14 – 21 days
2. Develop a strategic plan for diversity.	• Diversity Coordinator • Senior Leadership • CEO • Outside consultant as needed. • Legal counsel.	Provide a structured and detailed approach to diversity.	14 – 21 days
3. Conduct key stakeholder analysis.	• Executive Leadership Team • Board of Directors • Employees.	Identify the level of support for the diversity strategic plan.	7 – 14 days
4. Obtain approval of diversity strategic plan.	• Senior Leadership Team • Board of Directors.	Obtain final approval to go forward with implementing the strategic plan.	7 – 10 days
5. Develop a diversity training program.	• Executive Leadership Team • Diversity Coordinator • Human Resources representative • Outside consultants as needed.	Establish a program to increase diversity awareness.	14 – 21 days
6. Conduct diversity training with all employees and key stakeholders.	• Executive Leadership Team • Employees • Outside consultants if needed. • Financial support from the organization • Executive champion • Various training resources.	Provide diversity and sensitivity training to all employees.	30 – 60 days
7. Conduct issue-oriented surveys following the diversity training.	• Diversity Coordinator • Executive Leadership Team • Executive champion • Employees.	Solicit feedback about diversity following completion of the in-house training.	7–10 days
8. Design new total rewards and work-life programs based on feedback from employees and other key stakeholders.	• Diversity Coordinator • Senior leadership team • Human Resources representatives • Outside consultants if appropriate • Financial support from the organization depending on program package.	Provide programs and approaches which will promote and address diversity issues.	90–120 days

FIGURE 31 Sample Action Plan for Cultural Diversity (Continued)

Action(s)	Resources	Expected Outcome(s)	Timetable
9. Develop a plan for communicating the new diversity program and the work-life approaches.	• Diversity Coordinator • Executive champion • Senior Leadership Team • Employees • Outside communication consultant if needed • Legal consultant.	Have a structured plan for communicating diversity to all key stakeholders.	14 – 21 days
10. Evaluate the impact of the program.	• Diversity Coordinator • Executive Leadership Team • Key stakeholder assessment • Employees	Evaluate the success of the program on the employee participants and the organization. Develop monitoring tools, such as scorecards, for the program.	Ongoing

organization. The issue-oriented survey is an excellent tool for keeping the employee connected to the organization.

These elements are important to any culturally focused program. Appendix C provides a sample policy on job sharing and work sharing. Notice how the five elements have been integrated into each policy. The work-sharing policy clearly defines the difference between voluntary and involuntary work sharing. This is an important distinction because involuntary work sharing is simply a method to reassign an individual to another job. Finally, Figure 32 provides two examples of cultural approaches that have been aligned with the environment. The first involves flexible scheduling — this allows employees to work varying shifts to be readily available to their families. The second is a spot recognition program – this rewards positive workplace contributions that delight internal and external customers. Note that the environmental components support and give structure to the cultural approach. This ensures that the cultural approach has the infrastructure element it needs to be successful.

Branding Environment Programs

The last component in linking the culture with the environment is to market the programs to all key stakeholders. This is communicating the program in new and inventive ways. The best approach is to develop a "brand" that positively reinforces the program. For example, a customer service approach might look like the following:

Brand: "Our employees are GOLDEN."

Cultural Approach: A new spot recognition program called: "Go for the GOLD."

FIGURE 32 Aligning Culture with Environment

Cultural Approach	Environment Component(s)
Flexible Scheduling	
• Addresses needs of single parent household	• Policy on flexible staffing in place
• Addresses needs of student workers	• Jobs redesigned to accommodate staffing
	• Flexible scheduling incorporated into the organization's recruitment program
	• Cafeteria benefit plans offered to address the needs of the employee who works flexible schedules
	• Communication plan adopted to inform employees of the program's availability and potential impact
Spot Recognition	
• Rewards positive work contributions and workplace attitudes	• Policy on spot recognition developed
	• Recognition awards offered to employees
• Promotes teamwork and employee acceptance	• Recognition scorecard created to monitor the program's success
	• Recognition committee formed to champion the program

Environmental Component: The awarding of GOLD cards to employees who provide excellent customer service. The GOLD card can be converted to a cash prize or be used in conjunction with the performance evaluation.

Branding should be used to increase buy-in with the program from employees and key stakeholders. It should not be used as a cutesy marketing technique that has no tie in with the program. Figure 33 provides a sample checklist for creating a program brand. The checklist should be used to create a fun and appropriate brand that everyone can support. A brand should never offend or single out any individual group of employees. Humorous approaches should be tested with an objective audience before using them. In some cases, the organization may want to use an outside consultant to help create the program brand.

It is important that as we align culture with environment that we do not create a value conflict. The next chapter discusses how to identify potential value conflicts and how to incorporate them in a positive manner.

FIGURE 33 Sample Checklist for Creating a Program Brand

- ☐ Use positive and upbeat terms.
- ☐ Avoid trite and overused words.
- ☐ Test the brand with an employee focus group.
- ☐ Test humorous approaches on an objective audience.
- ☐ Never use vulgar or suggestive language to describe the brand.
- ☐ Use words that will effectively tie in the program with the brand.
- ☐ Do not take another organization's brand without permission.
- ☐ Make sure the brand accurately describes the program or plan being offered.
- ☐ Avoid brand names that might offend or alienate the key stakeholders.
- ☐ Integrate the brand with the company's logo or identity if possible.
- ☐ Use a brand name that is easily understood and remembered.
- ☐ Make sure the brand name does not undermine the goal of the program.

Dealing with Value Conflicts 5

Identifying Value Conflicts

Values are what we believe to be important and meaningful. Each person comes into an organization with his or her set of values and beliefs. The culture, like the individual, also promotes and supports certain values. A problem occurs when the individual's values conflict with the organizational values. When this happens, cognitive dissonance can occur. Cognitive dissonance is a psychological term that refers to the "discomfort created and felt as a result of a discrepancy between what we believe and what conflicting information is presented." This often occurs when employees try to accommodate their values with those of the organization. The result can be stressful and psychologically harmful.

Teachers and nurses have long been subjected to value conflicts and cognitive dissonance. Teachers are sometimes asked to provide quality education at the lowest possible cost. Without assistance from the educational system, teachers are forced to personally supplement needed resources to provide what they believe to be quality education. Nurses are often faced with the dilemma of providing quality patient care or leaving work early to satisfy the organization's need to keep costs down. The potential for value conflicts is possible in all organizations.

Figure 34 provides examples of potential conflicts between personal values and those enacted values of the organization. The policies, procedures, practices and programs of the organization impact the enacted values. Look at the potential conflict in Figure 34 between the personal value of commitment to family versus the organization's practice of working mandatory overtime. By having mandatory overtime, the organization will create cognitive dissonance with employees and eventually force them to look elsewhere for employment.

The organization must nurture positive personal values rather than trying to create an environment built on fear and doubt. Those personal values presented in Figure 34 are merely the tip of the iceberg to what employees can positively bring to the organization. The organization should review its own enacted values on an annual basis to protect against value conflicts. We will discuss in Chapter 7 the importance of conducting annual cultural surveys and policy audits. These two tools can help prevent value conflicts between the employee and the organization.

FIGURE 34 Potential Value Conflicts

Personal Value(s)	Organization's Enacted Value(s)	Organizational Practice(s)
Commitment to family outcomes	Commitment to overtime	Mandatory
		Inflexible policy on attendance.
High belief in quality	High profit motivation	Bottom-line driven.
		Compensation systems that reward quantity and low-cost work approaches.
		Output-focused productivity programs.
Strong ethical beliefs	Least path of resistance	Questionable ethical practices by leaders and the organization.
		No "Code of Conduct" in place.
		Total rewards programs based on unethical and questionable standards.
Equality for everyone	Structured workforce	Diversity is not evident in the workplace.
		Policies do not support diversity and equal access.
		Total rewards programs focus on the ethic but do not support work-life strategies.
Strong sense of loyalty	Tenure not valued	High turnover.
		Long-term service is not valued in the total rewards programs.
		Few opportunities for growth or promotion.

Action Point

Some actions, such as mandatory overtime, are necessary at times when managing a work group. Figure 34 is not meant to imply that some of these actions are not necessary at times. When they become an ongoing way of managing, it can impact the culture and the employee's personal values. A valuable tip for the manager is to maintain an awareness of how his or her actions impact the employee on an ongoing basis. I highly recommend using the issue-oriented survey to keep a handle on what is happening. It involves asking the employee two or three questions regarding morale of the department or unit. No manager can or should try to please employees all the time. It is the job of the manager, regardless of his or her personal style of leadership, to maintain a reasonably positive and productive work environment. Managers should try to seek methods to provide employees with a "coping mechanism" when conditions are less than ideal. An example of a coping mechanism is to offer a day off with pay or some special recognition when the employee has worked overtime for an extended period. If the manager is unethical, it becomes important for the employee to report such practices. If the organization chooses not to correct the problem, the employee is faced with possibly leaving the organization either voluntarily or involuntarily if the ethical dilemma is too great for the employee to handle. These are real-world decisions that employees and managers face every day in trying to cope with the dynamic nature of organizational culture.

Creating a Value Culture

In Figure 3 (in Chapter 1), values were listed as an important component of culture. There was a differentiation made between espoused and shared values. Espoused values are those organizational values that are communicated publicly but may not be shared by the organizational members. Creating a value culture takes more than just communicating value statements to employees. It involves buy-in from all key stakeholders. This buy-in can be achieved by systematically crafting the core values of the organization based on the input of all key stakeholders. Core values represent the organization's beliefs, attitudes, norms and behavioral system. In general, core values represent what the organization believes to be most important to its identity and long-term success. Examples of core values include:

- High commitment to ethical practices in all business transactions
- Respect for the privacy of the individual
- High commitment to quality and service
- Strong emphasis on teamwork
- Being accountable for work results
- High commitment to compassion and integrity
- Fostering a harmonious and respectful work environment.

Core values should be encompassed into the cultural profile that was developed in Chapter 3. Besides core values, two additional conditions are necessary to create a "value culture:"

Valuing everyone equally: Valuing everyone means sincerely treating all organizational members with equal respect and dignity. This includes showing the individual who values family the same respect as the individual who values spending time at work.

Making everyone feel valued: The outcome for this condition is creating value from within the organization. The organization creates internal value by recognizing the contributions and respecting the opinions of all its members.

Leadership plays a major role in creating a value culture. Leaders should follow the following three steps to foster a value-driven culture:

- **Step 1: Model behaviors that value the individual and the work team.**
  - Acknowledge the unique contributions of all employees.
  - Treat employees with dignity and respect.
  - Display a high level of emotional intelligence and personal control.
- **Step 2: Coach and develop employees to create a learning environment.**
  - Seek to reinforce positive work behaviors.
  - Provide employees with the information and resources to do their jobs effectively.
  - Jointly develop with the employee his or her developmental goals.
- **Step 3: Help employees better manage work and personal life objectives.**
  - Provide work-life programs that help employees better manage work and home.
  - Offer unique staffing alternatives as permitted. Some examples include shorter work weeks, condensed work schedules, job sharing and work sharing.
  - Determine how major work initiatives will impact employees before implementing them.

The leader must be tuned into the employee's needs. This can be achieved by asking employees what they need to be successful. The feedback from employees will surprise many leaders. Employees are seeking ways to balance work and home. If the organization can help the employee achieve this balance, the employee will feel valued. As discussed, this feeling of being valued is an important condition in creating a value culture.

The leaders must also display a high level of emotional intelligence in how they interact in high-stress situations. Employees watch how leaders respond and tend to model their behavior from them. Finally, leaders should develop and coach employees to help them reach personal and work objectives.

Employees must also be involved in creating a value culture. After soliciting input from the employee, it is important to get his or her commitment to creating and maintaining a value culture. Figure 35 is a sample pledge similar to the "Code of Conduct" in Appendix B that asks for the employee to commit to a value culture. Simplicity is the key in getting employees to commit to value. The value pledge in Figure 35 is simple and easily understood. These elements are important to building the value culture.

Leaders must communicate this pledge as an important first step to creating a value culture. By asking employees to post the pledge at their workstation, it emphasizes the importance of their commitment to creating value in their work experience.

Ensuring 'Organizational Fit'

It is important to ensure that a new employee is a good "organizational fit." To be a good organizational fit, the individual must possess some of the values promoted by the organization. Figure 34 listed some potential value conflicts for the employee. There is also the same potential for value conflicts for the organization. What if the organization makes a bad hiring decision? It can have a major impact on the organization as well as the individual's department or work group. This is why legally screening an individual with values that do not match the organization makes good business sense. In this case, a legal screen does not involve discriminating on the basis of gender, race, disability, religion or other unique characteristic. It involves matching the individual's values with the organization to avoid cognitive dissonance. The use of the "behavioral interview" will help the organization achieve a value match. This type of interview asks open-ended questions regarding personal and cultural values. The answers help paint a personal profile of the potential employee. Figure 36 provides some sample behavioral questions that focus on personal and cultural values. Notice how these responses can be used to determine if the individual will be a good organizational fit. To avoid any accusations of discrimination, it is important to ask all applicants the same questions.

FIGURE 35 **Sample Value Pledge**

1. I pledge to VALUE OTHERS in all of my daily interactions.
2. I pledge to support the CORE VALUES of the organization.
3. I pledge to be guided by the principle that everyone provides VALUE AND WORTH to the organization and to my work experience.

_____   _____
Employee's Signature   Date

Note: Please post this pledge at your workstation to remind you of your commitment.

FIGURE 36 Sample Behavioral Questions

1. What core values guide your work behavior?

   Please be specific: _____

   _____

2. What words do you associate with feeling personally valued?

   Elaborate: _____

   _____

3. What do you value most in a working environment?

   Please be descriptive: _____

   _____

4. What type of leadership style do you prefer? Why?

   Style of leadership: _____

   _____

   Reason(s): _____

   _____

5. How do you value others in the workplace?

   Please provide some examples: _____

   _____

6. Do you prefer to work alone or in teams?

   Please explain why you answered the way you did: _____

   _____

7. How can an organization show value to its employees?

   Be specific: _____

   _____

8. What if your supervisor asked you to do something that compromised your personal values? Would you still do it?

   Please be specific: _____

   _____

9. Do you feel like you can empathize with others in the workplace?

   Please provide an example of when you showed empathy in the workplace:

   _____

   _____

10. What would you do if you saw someone harassing or mistreating one of your coworkers?

    Please be specific: _____

    _____

    _____

The behavioral interview is one of several tools that can be used to determine organizational fit. The following list provides some additional methods and tools that can be used to assess organizational fit:

- **"Walk-Abouts"** — Have the applicant tour the physical plant and ask potential co-workers about the organization's culture.
- **Cultural profile** — Have the applicant review the cultural profile to determine if his or her values are comparable to the organization.
- **Cultural goals** — Have the applicant review and respond to the organization's cultural goals.
- **Mission and vision statements** — Review these documents with the applicant and ask how he or she feels about the content.
- **Web site review** — Have the applicant review the organization's Web site to determine how the work environment functions.
- **Leadership interview(s)** — Have the applicant meet with several organizational leaders to discuss the culture and environment.

Screening applicants to determine organizational fit can be time consuming and thought provoking. However, if the organization is truly committed to creating a value culture, it is essential to hire the right individual for the job.

Integrating Values with Total Rewards

When an organization seeks to develop value-driven programs that provide rewards to employees, it must first determine what really matters. Again, the issue-oriented survey can provide a quick glimpse at what is important to employees. Figure 37 provides three open-ended questions that can be used to help frame value-driven programs.

FIGURE 37 Sample Issue-Oriented Survey

1. What do you value most about your work experience?
   Please elaborate: _____

2. What core values help you guide your personal and work life?
   List of values: _____

3. How can the organization assist you in balancing work life with your home life?
   Please be specific: _____

The issue-oriented survey is easy to administer and analyze. It can be distributed as a payroll stuffer, a link on the organization's Web site, voice driven on a confidential hot line or mailed to employees and returned anonymously to the HR department. The feedback can be used to help design unique rewards programs.

What follows are examples of total rewards programs that attempt to link employee values:

- **Alternative Work Arrangements link to Family Values**
  - Flexible work schedules
  - Compressed work weeks
  - Job sharing
  - Telecommuting
  - Voluntary work sharing
  - Reduced work hours
  - Rotating shifts to accommodate the employee's family needs.
- **Community Involvement links to Community Caring**
  - Paid time to serve on the boards of human services agencies in the community
  - Paid time off to attend school or personal functions of children or other loved ones
  - Loaned executive programs that pay the manager to work in community agencies (e.g., United Way, Red Cross, Salvation Army)
  - Organizational fundraisers for local and national disasters chaired by employees
  - Donor programs in which the organization donates to employees' favorite charity.
- **Employee Involvement links to Employee Empowerment**
  - Suggestion programs
  - Serving on total quality improvement teams to review work processes
  - Soliciting of input on a regular basis from employees
  - Company-sponsored events, planned by employees, that address their unique interests.
- **Health and Wellness link to Valuing the Well-Being of the Employee**
  - On-site health fitness centers
  - Employee health fairs
  - On-site employee health program
  - Safety suggestion program
  - Safety incentive plans
  - Smoking cessation programs

- Weight loss programs on site
- Discounts on group health coverage granted to employees with healthy lifestyles
- Health education promoting healthy lifestyles.

Some of these total rewards programs can be linked to employee values. An excerpt of the excellent study about flexible work schedules, conducted by the Alliance for Work-Life Progress (AWLP), in conjunction with The Regional Research Institute for Human Services, is provided in Chapter 8. It is noteworthy that 9 percent of all part-time jobs in Australia for 2003 involved some type of job sharing, according to the Australian Bureau of Statistics. Organizations must continue to respond to employee values to provide the type of environment that is free of cognitive dissonance and value conflict.

We are now ready to link some of these employee values with the customer's needs. The next chapter will discuss how to link culture to the customer value chain.

Developing a Cultural Chain 6

The Customer Value Chain

Customer service involves meeting the internal and external customers' needs and expectations. The distinction between internal and external customers is important to note because both are impacted by the customer's value chain. The customer value chain is represented in Figure 38. The traditional customer value chain has been refined to integrate customer needs with the culture. Customer needs are identified in the top half of the chain. The necessary activities to fulfill each customer need are identified in the middle section of the chain. For example, "marketing and consumer education" include the following key activities:

- Providing basic product/service information
- Persuading the customer to purchase the product or service
- Determining if the product/service matches the customer's needs (e.g., customer fit)
- Building a customer base to ensure repeat purchases (e.g., customer loyalty).

The dashed boxes in Figure 38 align customer needs with the culture. Some of the same activities used to meet the external customers' needs are used to meet the cultural needs of the organization. For example, the following are activities to "market and provide information" to the internal customer about culture:

- Communicating cultural and diversity goals

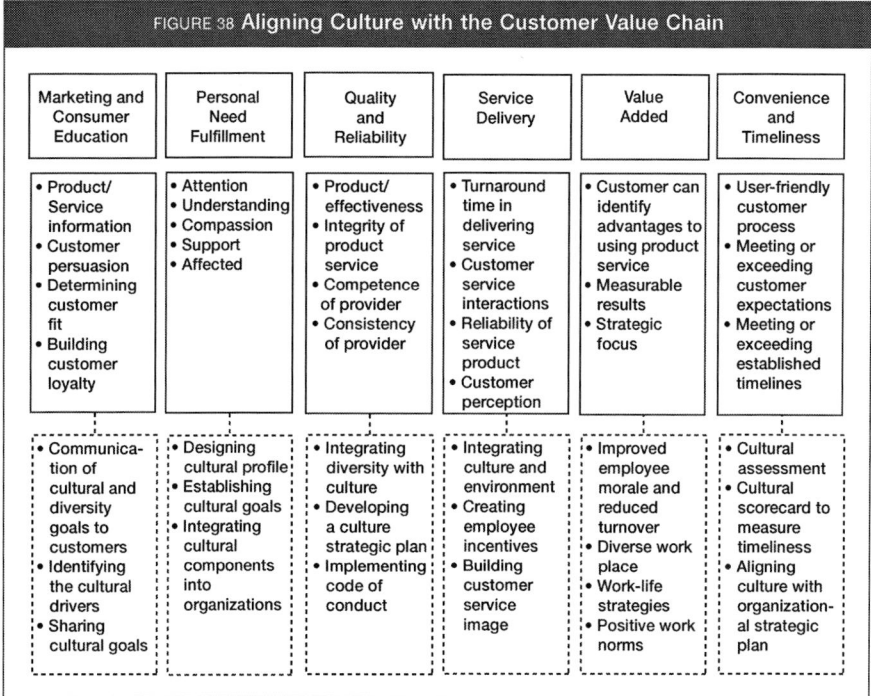

FIGURE 38 Aligning Culture with the Customer Value Chain

- Identifying cultural drivers and using them to shape the organization
- Sharing the cultural goals with external and internal customers.

Aligning customer needs with culture is essential if the organization is to be successful. Too often, we are too concerned about the external customer and forget about the employee. In *Fortune's* "Top 100 Companies to Work for," it was obvious that employee customers were just as important as the external customer to these highly successful organizations. Wegmans, for example, stressed that when employees are happy, customers will be treated better and ultimately will have their needs met. When a company invests in work-life programs, it results in creating a culture built on respect and consideration. This will, in turn, be instilled in how the employee treats all customers. Customers' experience will be positively enhanced and their "culture of value" boosted without much financial investment on the part of the organization.

Cultural needs and key stakeholders have been discussed at length in this publication. The term "key stakeholder" has been used repeatedly. Who are these key stakeholders? These individuals must be supportive and knowledgeable about the importance of aligning the culture with the customer. Figure 39 provides a sample checklist to determine these key stakeholders.

This checklist should be used by individuals directly involved in making cultural change. For example, the HR executive or his or her representative should use this checklist to determine who are the key stakeholders who need to be informed of any cultural change. The executive leadership team, or an appointed executive, should use the checklist when developing the cultural profile or making changes in the strategic direction of the organization.

FIGURE 39 Checklist for Identifying Key Stakeholders

Individual or Group (e.g., Employee, Manager, Customer)

- ☐ Has control over financial or people resources
- ☐ Has direct involvement in developing cultural or customer strategies
- ☐ Has direct involvement in ensuring cultural alignment is effectively communicated
- ☐ Will be directly or indirectly impacted by the aligning of culture with the environment
- ☐ Will receive formal education or training regarding cultural alignment
- ☐ Is major decision maker in approving culture and customer strategies
- ☐ Is actively involved in implementing any cultural or customer changes
- ☐ Is involved in monitoring the alignment of culture and the customer on an ongoing basis
- ☐ Has direct impact on the success of aligning culture with customer goals
- ☐ Manages certain aspects of the culture and the customer

The checklist refers to an individual stakeholder who may need to be informed. It also helps identify groups that have a significant impact on the culture such as board of directors or donors for a nonprofit organization. The checklist's purpose is to determine who these stakeholders are and then utilize the tool in Figure 40 to alignment.

A "checkmark" on any of the listed items probably indicates that the individual is a key stakeholder. Examples of key stakeholders include:

- Customers
- Employees
- Managers
- Executives
- Vendors
- Board members.

Remember a stakeholder is any individual who is key to the success of a program or service that has been developed for customers. After identifying those key internal and external stakeholders, it is important to assess their level of support and knowledge. A simple scale from 1 to 5, with a score of "5" being high, can be used to determine the level of knowledge and support of the key stakeholder for cultural initiatives. Figure 40 provides a simple rating of key stakeholders. This rating should be used to determine what actions, if any, are needed to gain the key stakeholder's support and increase his or her knowledge regarding cultural initiatives. These identified actions should be incorporated into an action plan similar to one developed in Figure 31 in Chapter 4.

The example in Figure 40 could be the implementation of any cultural initiative. There are no generic actions for how to deal with individual stakeholders. Each individual or group must be dealt with in accordance with its current knowledge base of and support level for the proposed initiative.

Remember vendors are important stakeholders in the customer value chain. Vendors provide products and services that create customer value. They impact quality and reliability, in particular, but also may bring new approaches to cultural initiatives. A good relationship with the vendor can positively impact the organization's ability to adapt to customer and employee needs. Finally, the actions identified in Figure 40 would obviously need to be expanded to fully address the stakeholder's needs.

Defining Customer Value

Customer value is contingent upon how the customer perceives and assesses what is received versus what must be given in return. Figure 41 provides a pictorial equation of this definition. Customers are simply looking to gain more from the relationship

FIGURE 40 Assessing Key Stakeholders

Key Stakeholder	Current Level of Knowledge Low 1 2 3 4 5 High	Current Level of Support Low 1 2 3 4 5 High	Action(s)
Employee	1	1	Diversity training
Manager	2	3	Seek input
Customers	1	3	Customer marketing
Vendors	1	4	Partnering with suppliers

with the organization than what they "pay" in terms of money, time or commitment.

To create a positive value for the equation in Figure 41, the organization must be willing to address the six customer needs identified in the top six boxes in Figure 38. Those needs include:

- **Marketing and consumer education:** The educational needs of the external and internal customer must be equally addressed. Culture must also be communicated to employees and external customers if real value is to be created.
- **Personal need fulfillment:** The importance of creating a cultural profile is clearly evident. It ensures the organization can match its customer goals with its cultural goals. The integration of cultural components is necessary to fulfill customer needs.
- **Quality and reliability:** The external customer's preference for high-quality products and services must be merged with its cultural strategic goals. At this stage, the Code of Conduct helps frame the organization's culture to deliver on its customer needs.
- **Service delivery:** Total rewards is integrated to provide incentives for excellent customer service. Notice the incentives are created to reward excellent service to internal and external customers.
- **Added value:** The focus on the internal customer is to address specific needs through such approaches as work-life strategies and diversity. The external customer will benefit from receiving higher quality services and products, as the employee is able to focus their efforts on productivity rather than self-servant issues.
- **Convenience and timeliness:** This component seeks to measure the effectiveness of delivering value in a timely and convenient manner. Aside from measuring service delivery times, this area also focuses on meeting

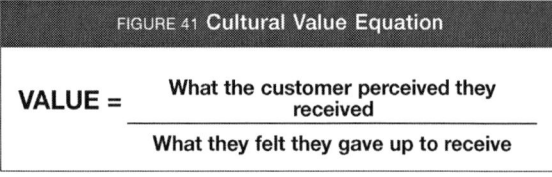

FIGURE 41 Cultural Value Equation

$$\text{VALUE} = \frac{\text{What the customer perceived they received}}{\text{What they felt they gave up to receive}}$$

cultural initiatives. By focusing on the employee customer as well, the impetus for completing timely services will be present. Conducting a cultural assessment will determine how committed the organization is to its internal and external customers.

The bottom line is that customer value is dramatically impacted by the culture and how it is absorbed into service delivery. If employees are sidetracked by a weak culture built on the "bottom line," the results can be disastrous for the organization. It is virtually impossible to build external customer value without first building a strong culture to support it. This is why Four Seasons or The Ritz-Carlton can charge and receive an extra monetary value for its services. Both organizations are committed to empowering their employees to offer superior customer service. In turn, the employees in both organizations are treated more like strategic partners rather than "hired help." The successful organization is aware of the importance of culture and the need to effectively manage it.

Matching Culture with Customer Service Goals

Figure 42 illustrates the circular process of linking culture with customer service. Perception helps produce a positive or negative linkage between culture and the customer. If perception is negative, the relationship must be repaired before developing customer goals. For the internal customer, the negative perceptions can be determined by conducting a cultural survey. (See Appendix D.) Use the survey results to positively address issues and concerns. For the external customer, the organization must ask for feedback or use an impartial method for surveying customer acceptance. The customer feedback then can be used to develop customer goals. The organization must link the customer goals with the culture. The following example shows how an organization would link a customer goal with the culture.

In this example, linkage between the customer goal and the culture was established by using various cultural aspects. Once linkage has been determined, the cultural linkage must be validated. Methods for validating this linkage include conducting a cultural audit with senior leadership; measuring cultural impact via scorecard or other statistical tools; and conducting a policy audit to determine if the environment is supporting the cultural and customer goals. (See Appendix E.)

Once linkage has been established, the next step in the process is to evaluate customer and cultural linkage on an ongoing basis. This evaluation is a continuous process. This process includes evaluating such aspects as customer service goals, cultural goals, training outcomes, policy reviews and ongoing statistical measurement. It is a comprehensive process that should be coordinated and carefully managed. The perceived customer relationship, both for the internal and external customer, can change over time. For this reason, the evaluation process must be carefully scrutinized. As perceptions change, the organization must make appropriate cultural adjustments to ensure this linkage remains positive. Cultural strategy and the environment must adapt to the changing needs of the customer. This could mean realigning cultural goals with customer goals and revisiting the cultural profile to ensure it still represents what the organization wants to follow.

We are now ready to pursue ongoing cultural development to protect and preserve the culture and the environment. This ongoing development process must be carefully developed and communicated. The next chapter provides some invaluable tools for making this a successful process.

FIGURE 41 **Customer Goal versus Cultural Aspects**

Customer Goal	Cultural Aspects
The organization will improve customer satisfaction by 10% during the next 12 months	• Cultural profile supports excellent customer service. • The cultural scorecard focuses on how the culture impacts customer service. • The work environment has implemented customer service training with all employees.

Ongoing Cultural Development 7

Cultural Surveys

The organization should conduct an annual cultural survey with all employees. The purpose of the survey is to determine the impact of culture and environment on the employee's work experience. Survey results should be widely shared and discussed by senior leadership. The results of the survey should also be discussed with employees in feedback sessions or written summaries. Additional feedback from employees is necessary to verify the feedback from the survey. Employee focus groups can be used to discuss and solicit additional input about survey data. Figure 43 identifies the four key areas to include in the cultural survey.

The four components in Figure 43 can be used to create a cultural survey similar to the one provided in Appendix D. It is important to have a "standalone" cultural survey, which is identified as separate from any other employee opinion survey. The cultural survey comes with the same caution as other employee opinion surveys. If the organization does not plan to use the results, it is a waste of time. The survey is not a "feel-good" tool but a resource for building a strong and supportive culture. The results should be used to develop action plans to address issues and concerns. Employees should be informed about any changes that come about as a result of the survey.

The survey is a valuable tool to determine if the organization's environment supports the organization's culture. It solicits input about the effectiveness of policies and procedures and how they are administered. The final question of the survey is open ended to allow employees to express their views about the organization's culture and the work environment. From this feedback, the organization can determine if it needs to develop new cultural strategies and implement new total rewards programs. The length of the survey should be limited to no more than 25 questions.

In the sample survey provided in Appendix D, the survey includes 20 questions and one open-ended question at the end. If the organization asks too many questions, the results tend to be redundant and include very little additional information. Employees should be encouraged to participate in the survey but participation should not be mandatory. Mandatory surveys send the wrong cultural message. Employees must be told the survey is a valuable tool for them to give feedback about the organization. Senior leadership should communicate their support of the survey and a willingness to use the results to better the organization.

> FIGURE 43 **Key Areas of a Cultural Survey**
>
> 1. **Culture and Personal Values**
>   - Communication of cultural goals
>   - Matching culture with the employee's personal beliefs and values
>   - Work-life balance
> 2. **Cultural Diversity**
>   - Organization's stand on diversity
>   - Diversity training
>   - Equal access for employees
> 3. **Environment**
>   - Application of policies and rules
>   - Reporting workplace violations
>   - Job opportunities
> 4. **Job Satisfaction and Workplace Value**
>   - Job satisfaction level for the employee
>   - Teamwork and workplace cooperation
>   - Organization's reputation in the community
>   - Employee morale

Action Point

The cultural survey should be used to do a "gut check" of how the employee feels about the culture on an ongoing basis. The survey can also be used to help formulate the cultural profile discussed in Chapter 3. It is important that the cultural survey be conducted at least annually to determine the employee's commitment and thoughts about the current culture.

Policy Audits

The organization should conduct an audit of all its policies and practices at least annually. The audit will help the organization determine if its policies and practices support the culture. There are three other reasons for conducting annual audits:

1. **Legal compliance:** Each policy and practice should comply with applicable laws and regulatory guidelines. This is particularly true for cultural diversity. The organization must maintain a work environment that provides equal access to all employees and applicants.

2. **Cultural implications:** An audit will help determine if the policy or practice has any impact on the organization's culture. For example, a restrictive work scheduling policy that does not allow the employee any time to address personal life needs.
3. **Applicability and intent:** It must be determined if the policy is still applicable to the organization's needs. It must also be determined if the original intent of the policy or practice is still being followed or has it been abandoned. In short, there are too many policies and practices that are obsolete or need to be revised to be in step with the culture and environment.

The audit is a valuable tool but the results must be shared with senior leadership for it to be meaningful. Figure 44 provides a checklist to follow when conducting the policy and practice audit.

It is important to schedule the audit in advance to ensure it will be conducted annually by an impartial individual(s). In some cases, this may mean using an outside consultant. The format of the audit should be easy to follow and use. Appendix E provides a sample policy audit. This sample audit provides a simplistic approach to determining if the policy is still relevant to the culture and the environment. The second part of the audit is open ended to allow for recommendations to be formulated and shared with applicable departments and senior leadership. The audit results should be communicated first with affected departments and individuals to assure that interpretations of the policy and practice have not been misrepresented. The final audit results should be in writing and presented to senior leadership for review. After carefully reviewing the results with senior leadership, a plan of action should be developed to address deficiencies in policy and practice administration. One of the recommendations from an audit may be to eliminate a policy or practice. As stated previously, some

---

FIGURE 44 Checklist for Conducting a Policy and Practice Audit

☐ Schedule the audit.
☐ Audit all policies and practices at least annually.
☐ Use impartial individuals to conduct the audit.
☐ Provide an easy-to-use format for conducting the audit.
☐ Review the entire policy and practice to determine intent.
☐ Determine if the policy is still applicable to the organization.
☐ Review compliance with the policy and practice.
☐ Review the audit results with the appropriate department and individual.
☐ Document the audit findings in writing.
☐ Make recommendations about how to improve or revise the policy or practice.
☐ Develop a plan for communicating audit results to key stakeholders.
☐ Present final audit results to senior leadership for review.

policies and practices simply have outlived their usefulness and are no longer appropriate for the organization. Finally, the audit results, and any corresponding changes, must be carefully communicated to employees and key stakeholders. The audit should be viewed as positive and necessary to maintaining a supportive and strong culture.

Readiness Assessment

After the survey and audit, the organization may determine that new programs must be developed to address the identified needs and issues. Before embarking on any new program, the organization should conduct a "readiness assessment" with its senior leaders and managers. Figure 45 provides a sample readiness assessment for a new flexible scheduling program.

The first question in the readiness assessment is key to developing any new culturally driven program. If top leadership refuses to support the new program, the assessment does not need to continue. It is important to have the support of senior leadership before proceeding with implementing any new program. Question 8 in

FIGURE 45 Readiness Assessment

1. Does the organization have the commitment from senior leadership (managers) to offer flexible scheduling strategies? ☐ Yes   ☐ No
2. Is the organization committed to soliciting input from employees, managers and other key stakeholders about flexible scheduling strategies? ☐ Yes   ☐ No
3. Is the organization willing to commit financial and human resources to a flexible staffing program? ☐ Yes   ☐ No
4. Is the organization willing to communicate the program to employees?
   ☐ Yes   ☐ No
5. Is there a commitment to train managers and supervisors about flexible staffing arrangements? ☐ Yes   ☐ No
6. Will flexible staffing allow the organization to still be able to appropriately address workload needs? ☐ Yes   ☐ No
7. Are managers and supervisors supportive of using flexible staffing arrangements?
   ☐ Yes   ☐ No
8. Do employees view flexible staffing as an important element of their work experience? ☐ Yes   ☐ No
9. Is the organization willing and able to implement a new program at this point in its operation? ☐ Yes   ☐ No
10. Does the organization have the ability to monitor the impact of flexibility on the organization? ☐ Yes   ☐ No

Figure 45 may at first glance appear to be out of place. However, this question is asking senior leadership and managers if they think employees view the program as important. This is an important distinction to make because it may also be an additional indicator of the value that the manager believes the program to have for his or her employees. If the readiness assessment has three or more "no" responses, the program is probably not ready to be implemented. Each question in the assessment tool provides a guide about how to proceed with making the organization ready. For example, a "no" response to Question 5 could prove detrimental to the program's success. When implementing a flexible-staffing program, it is vital that supervisors and managers be trained on how to use it effectively. Finally, the readiness assessment helps the organization to plot a course of action rather than just trying to "fix" the organization. It helps identify areas to address and who must be involved if the program is to be effective.

Soliciting and Maintaining Management Support

Management support must be solicited and maintained to give credibility to the program or approach. In Chapter 4, we discussed the importance of having an executive champion. It is paramount that an executive champion be identified early in the development process. An executive champion provides unquestionable support and clout. This is important especially for culturally driven programs, which are often seen as "soft" by top management. The executive champion will be the front person extolling the virtues of the new program or approach. An executive champion can drag other senior leaders along for the ride with his or her enthusiastic support. The executive champion also has the clout to help obtain financial support and human resources needed to implement the program.

The "star" is also an enthusiastic supporter who has a high commitment to the program's success. The star may be an informal leader who sees the new program or approach as improving work-life. The star may also be a manager who knows the new program will benefit employees and provide an important tool to help improve the work environment. Figure 46 identifies a checklist of elements needed to solicit and maintain management support for culturally driven programs and approaches.

Figure 24 in Chapter 3 provides a sample leadership assessment. A leadership assessment should be conducted early in the process to determine management support and create synergy. Managers should be provided with "talking points" that delineate how the new program/approach will be implemented. Talking points provide managers with valuable information, which they can use to give consistent information about the program/approach to their employees. Talking points answer the following questions:

1. What is being done?
2. Why is the program/approach being offered?

3. How will the program/approach be implemented?
4. Who is impacted by the new program/approach?
5. When will the new program/approach be implemented?

Talking points are more than just a script for managers to use when discussing the new program/approach with their employees. Talking points anticipate the information needs of the employees and make them available to managers first. This gives managers a chance to absorb the process and lend their support. Appendix F provides sample talking points for a cultural diversity program. It is also important to keep managers updated and trained on the new program/approach. This gives managers the confidence and knowledge about how to best use the program/approach. Individual and departmental successes should be featured in communications to other employees and managers. This helps to provide an organizational benchmark for how to best utilize the program/approach.

> **FIGURE 46 Checklist for Elements for Soliciting and Maintaining Management Support**
>
> ☐ Identify an executive champion.
> ☐ Involve senior leadership from the beginning.
> ☐ Identify stars and supporters.
> ☐ Assess leadership support early in the process.
> ☐ Continue to seek management input on an ongoing basis.
> ☐ Provide managers with "talking points" about new programs and changes.
> ☐ Update management training on how to effectively use the program/approach.
> ☐ Track organizational and departmental successes.
> ☐ Seek individual testimonials regarding program use.
> ☐ Create synergy by keeping the program/approach current and relevant.

Action Point

It is imperative to keep managers actively engaged in the cultural development process. A comprehensive orientation about the cultural development process should be provided to first-line supervisors and managers. Supervisors and managers should be encouraged to give their input how best to deliver the message to employees about cultural development. The purpose of "talking points" is to provide the first-line supervisors and managers with a written tool. The organization's responsibility does not stop with providing talking points. The first-line supervisor is critical to the success of any cultural development program. The ability of the first-line supervisor and manager to understand and embrace the program cannot be taken lightly. For some organizations, this means an investment in training supervisors and managers about how to facilitate effective employee meetings and how to effectively communicate to employees. The time spent preparing supervisors and manager is worth the investment because of the dramatic impact that these two groups have on employees and the culture in general. The organizations should not scrimp on preparing supervisors for this important task.

Finally, the program must be kept fresh and relevant by seeking input from its users and ensuring that the environment provides appropriate policies and procedures. This is why managers must be involved in the annual audit and survey process. Managers must have the knowledge of how they are doing and what they could be doing to improve. Involving managers is a continuous and necessary process. Without management support, it is impossible to provide viable and meaningful programs. The first-line manager is the individual whom employees rely on to give them reliable and accurate information. This can only be possible if the manager has accurate and reliable information from the beginning.

Ongoing Communication

Communication is the key element to ensuring that culturally driven programs/approaches will be absorbed into the environment. When the organization determines it is ready to implement a new program or approach, a comprehensive communication plan must be developed. The purpose of the plan is to identify what resources and actions should be taken to communicate the new program or approach. Figure 47 provides a detailed approach to building a communication plan.

The six-step process detailed in Figure 47 was used to develop the sample communication plan provided in Appendix G. The sample communication plan is for a cultural diversity program. It identifies excellent communication tools including employee meetings, focus groups, strategy teams and informational forums. The organization must rely on a variety of media, written and verbal approaches to communicate the importance of these programs.

In addition to developing a communication plan, the organization must develop communication objectives and key messages for the program/approach. Some examples of communication objectives include:

- Inform all key stakeholders about a new program, such as flexible scheduling as an example.
- Increase awareness of flexible staffing arrangements with all eligible employees.
- Provide training to managers and supervisors on how to effectively utilize flexible staffing arrangements.
- Obtain support for flexible staffing from all managers and eligible employees.

Key messages should be few and used to reinforce the program's content and communication objectives. Consider the following examples of key messages:

- Flexible scheduling helps the employee balance work with his or her personal life.
- Employees want the opportunity to adjust their work schedule when special needs arise.
- Training improves the understanding of how to manage a flexible scheduling arrangement.

> **FIGURE 47 Building a Communication Plan**
>
> **Step 1: Answer the following key questions before establishing a plan:**
> - Who will be impacted by the plan?
> - What is going to be communicated (e.g., new flexible scheduling program, a sexual harassment policy, diversity plan, etc.)?
> - Where are the stakeholders who need to hear the message (e.g., in multiple locations, departments, shifts, etc.)?
> - When do the stakeholders need to know the information?
> - Why do the stakeholders need to know?
> - How will we get the message to them?
>
> **Step 2: Identify what steps must be taken to communicate the message.**
> - Conduct employee meetings.
> - Provide survey feedback.
> - Announce a new program or approach.
> - Announce a new training program.
> - Communicate on an ongoing basis.
>
> **Step 3: Identify what action(s) to take.**
>
> **Step 4: Agree upon expected outcomes.**
>
> **Step 5: Identify what resources will be needed.**
>
> **Step 6: Establish timetable for completion.**

- Flexible scheduling is widely supported by senior leadership as a valuable work-life resource.

With objectives and key messages identified, the organization must identify the audience for the communication. The action plan similar to Figure 31 (Chapter 4) helps identify key stakeholders and resources. Other individuals needing communication include vendors, family members, board members and the external customer. The timetable for communicating a new culturally driven program can be extensive depending on the type of program being offered. A cultural diversity program can take up to six months to communicate depending on the size of the organization. While this may seem long, the communication requirements are much greater for culturally driven programs/approaches. These programs must be communicated continuously before the organization will accept and embrace them.

Ongoing communication is a challenge for culturally driven programs/approaches. Some organizations have used theme-based communication approaches including:

- **Cultural fairs** that seek to provide information about ethnic cultures and customs.

- **Community service thermometers** that are posted throughout the organization to show community involvement by employees and management.
- **Cultural events** aimed at fostering teamwork and fun (e.g., bass fishing tournament)
- **Health and wellness fairs** that focus on providing employees on-site health services and wellness information.
- **Work-life contests** between departments to reward efforts for effectively utilizing work-life strategies.

Theme-based approaches should be supplemented with other communication approaches. However, they do generate excitement about the culture and the programs.

Finally, ongoing communication must rely on a variety of media and approaches. Examples of media include:

- **Internet and intranet postings:** New programs and approaches can be featured on the organization's Web site.
- **Written updates:** Letters sent directly to the employee's home from the CEO or the human resources department.
- **Video:** This is an expensive media but does provide a consistent and accurate message. Only highly credible sources should be used if the organization is produced using employees or internal resources.
- **Posters and notices** must be in a conspicuous location to catch the attention of the employee. Some organizations have a central location for posting program announcement and events.
- **Employee handbooks:** Program content can be included in the employee handbook if provided. It is important to update the handbook as new programs are implemented.
- **Informational forums:** These forums are large, public information sessions for employees. Organizations with multiple sites will obviously need to hold off-site sessions.
- **Departmental meetings:** The manager can provide frequent program updates at regularly scheduled departmental meetings. This gives the employee an opportunity to ask questions within his or her support group.
- **Employee orientation:** New employees should be informed about culturally driven programs during orientation. This helps establish the perception the new employee will have about the culture and environment.

Ongoing communication must follow three very important principles:

1. **The communication should not overpower the program.**

   It is important to provide accurate and useful information. If the communication overpowers the intent of the program, the employee may fail to see the program's benefits. Advertising a product is different than providing cultural communication. The objective of cultural communication is to provide accurate and complete information as opposed to trying to sell a specific product.

2. **Avoid novel approaches that might offend.**

   Typical examples would be communication that incorporates humor and pokes fun at other cultures, community values or important organizational beliefs. The best way to avoid offensive communication is to test all communication approaches with an impartial audience before implementing the communication approach.

3. **The communication becomes part of the culture itself.**

   It is important to note that the approach used to communicate a new program becomes part of the culture and the environment. If the communication generates excitement and enthusiasm, the result will probably be positive acceptance by the organization's members and be embraced into the culture.

The final goal for any ongoing communication program is to keep the program relevant and valued. It is sometimes a significant challenge to communicate "soft programs" that focus on the culture or the environment. HR professionals must continue to assess the effectiveness of the communication with employees. If the communication no longer generates synergy, and promotes program utilization, it may need to be changed or eliminated. This represents an uphill battle but one that will reap benefits for the organization's culture.

This book has provided a comprehensive study of how culture and environment have a monumental impact on the organization. The goal was to give readers tools to assist them in managing these two important elements. There are some excellent examples of organizations that have diligently incorporated culture with their business strategy. Chapter 8 provides an unusual example of how one organization values its employees above its customers. Wegmans, the "best place to work for" in 2005 according to *Fortune*, has integrated culture and environment to create a highly respected and productive organization. Chapter 8 also provides an excerpt from a study about flexible work schedules conducted by the Alliance for Work-Life Progress (AWLP) and The Regional Research Institute for Human Services. This study reinforces the need to provide flexible work schedules as a viable work-life strategy.

Case Study

8

Wegmans Food Markets

Ownership: Wegmans is a privately held, family-owned company, founded in 1916 by the Wegman family. Robert Wegman is the chairman; his son, Danny, is the CEO; and granddaughter, Colleen, is the president.

Headquartered: The central offices are located in Rochester, N.Y. Wegmans operates 69 stores with 51 in New York, 10 in Pennsylvania, five in New Jersey, two in Virginia and one in Maryland.

Sales Revenues: $3.6 billion in 2004

Number of Employees: More than 35,000 people are employed by Wegmans.

Awards and Distinctions:

- Selected by *Fortune* as the "best company to work for" in 2005
- Selected every year since 1998 to *Fortune's* list of "Best Companies to Work for"
- The American Society for Training and Development selected Danny Wegman as the 2005 Champion of Workplace Learning and Performance
- Working Mother magazine named Wegmans to its list of "Best Companies for Working Mothers" for six consecutive years (1990-1995)
- A number of community excellence awards including:
  - The Corning Award for Excellence given to Robert Wegman for his commitment to the state of New York
  - The American Business Media's award for community service
  - Educational Achievement Award for outstanding contribution to education.

Wegmans has been one of America's most-honored employers for its commitment to its employees and to the communities it serves. Wegmans embodies the kind of strong corporate culture discussed in Chapter 1 of this publication. Wegmans is a diverse and adaptable culture, which focuses on the internal and external customer. This remarkable employer has built a successful organization by placing a high value on its organizational members. Its turnover is 6 percent, which is a fraction of the 19-percent norm for most grocer chains. Let's look at how Wegmans has achieved such monumental success.

Learning Culture

Wegmans has awarded $56 million in scholarships to more than 18,000 employees since the organization started the Wegmans Scholarship Program in 1984. About 2,500 students receive assistance each year to attend colleges and universities across the country. Wegmans also is committed to continuing education for its employees. It will send employees on site to such places as London, Paris or Italy to learn more about cheeses that they may offer in one of its supermarkets.

Wegmans never opens a store until it believes its employees are absolutely trained and ready to provide service. In 2003-2004, the company spent $5 million on training employees at one of its locations. It delayed opening this location until February 2004 even though opening it in November 2003 would have captured holiday revenue. This emphasis of development over dollars has helped attract highly qualified individuals outside of retail. Some of these individuals, such as Heather Pawlowski, came to Wegmans because of its commitment to development. Pawlowski, an electrical engineering graduate from Cornell, was trained on all aspects of grocer retail from baking bread to cutting meat. Pawlowski is now a vice president with Wegmans.

In 1987, Wegmans formed the Work-Scholarship to help reduce the dropout rate in the Rochester, N.Y., City School District. The program has more than 1,000 middle and high school students participate each year. This program illustrates Wegmans' commitment to education and also its commitment to the community.

Community Commitment

In addition to the Work-Scholarship program, Wegmans is a major contributor to the communities where stores are located. Every Wegmans store has a budget for community giving. Wegmans focuses its giving in four areas:

- Food for the needy
- Donations to neighborhood activities, such as community festivals
- Support to help young people become healthy, productive and independent adults
- Support for the United Way as an effective way to fund programs that make a difference.

Wegmans gave 15 million pounds of food to food banks in 2004. In 2004, the company received 3,600 letters from individuals asking them to open a Wegmans store in their community.

Merging Culture with Strategy

The Wegmans culture is blended into its business strategy. The company has had uncommon operating results for a grocer chain. The company margins have hovered around 7.5 percent, which is double what the big four grocer chains earn. A Wegmans store is an adventure for the grocery shopper. A typical Wegmans store has more than 60,000 products compared to more than 40,000 for most supermarkets. The size of a Wegmans store ranges from 80,000 to 130,000 square feet, which is three times the size of most supermarkets.

Each Wegmans store offers unique products and services, such as market cafes that offer take-out or in-store dining; a large diverse selection of cheeses; a wine shop; bakery; deli; a dry cleaner; video rentals; pharmacy; play centers for kids; food from around the world; an authentic French pastry shop; and various other unique amenities not often found in a supermarket.

Yet, with all of this variety, the employees provide the most unique element of the business strategy. Wegmans empowers its employees to solve customer concerns on the spot. This could mean having a Wegmans chef cook the Thanksgiving turkey because it could not fit in the oven instead of refunding money to an unhappy customer. But the empowerment is not limited to the external customer. Wegmans has created an environment that allows employees to make suggestions and changes, which will foster the success of the business. For example, one employee suggested a new product and it was implemented and used by Wegmans with great success. Wegmans encourages employee involvement and rewards and recognizes the employee for his or her contributions. One consultant noted in the *Fortune* article that the "Wegmans culture is bigger than Danny (Wegman) in the same way that Wal-Mart's became bigger than Sam (Walton)."

Customer Driven

Wegmans focuses on the internal and external customer. However, Wegmans is driven by the motto: "Employees first, customers second." Wegmans pays its employees at the high end of the market and offers excellent employee benefits programs. As an organization, Wegmans is guided by the following customer pledge:

> WE BELIEVE:
>
> At Wegmans, we believe that good people, working toward a common goal, can accomplish anything they set out to do.
>
> In this spirit, we set our goal to be the very best at *serving the needs of our customers*. Every action we take should be made with this in mind.
>
> We also believe that we can achieve our goal only if we *fulfill the needs of our own people*.
>
> To our customers and our people we pledge continuous improvement, and we make the commitment: *"Every day you get our best."*

This pledge has guided Wegmans culture and business strategy. Wegmans has been remarkably successful in a highly competitive industry. Yet, it is the commitment to culture and environment that has helped grow this success. About 6,000 employees, or almost 20 percent of the total workforce, have 10 or more years of service with Wegmans. Why such a commitment in an industry characterized by high turnover, low wages and poor employee morale? Wegmans values its employees and its customers equally. By valuing its employees, Wegmans has created a strong culture coupled with a supportive and compassionate work environment. Robert Wegman, Wegmans chairman, eloquently stated how this commitment to employees has paid big dividends: "I have never given away more than I got back."

This statement certainly indicates the value of strong leadership in building a supportive and strong culture. If leadership is committed to strong corporate values, this becomes the culture and values of its employees. The Wegmans culture will continue to stand out as an excellent model for other organizations to follow.

Appendices

Appendix A
Workplace Diversity Strategy

I. Diversity Statement
We value diversity by treating all organizational members with respect and dignity.

II. Definitions
- **Workplace diversity:** This involves creating an inclusive work environment that honors and integrates all individuals from various cultural backgrounds and perspectives into the organization. Perspectives are impacted by such diversity elements as age, race, color, ethnicity, gender, disability, religion, sexual orientation, language, geographic location and other unique characteristics.
- **Code of Conduct:** The organization has developed a Code of Conduct that delineates the organization's commitment to diversity. All employees must read and agree to uphold the values and components of this document.
- **Equal access:** All organizational members will have equal access to employment opportunities and other aspects of work life.
- **Employment equity:** A workplace that is free from harassment and discrimination of any kind. All employment decisions are based solely on merit.

III. Employee's Role
All employees must help create an environment where diversity is valued and respected. The employee will commit to the following:
- Treating all employees with respect and consideration
- Be open minded in all personal interactions
- Refuse to accept workplace harassment or discrimination
- Report violations of the Code of Conduct to the proper individual
- Ensure all employees can equally participate in the work process
- Identify and assist in addressing in barrier to workplace diversity.

IV. Leadership Role
Individuals in leadership positions have the following responsibilities in supporting workplace diversity:
- Actively support and encourage workplace diversity
- Lead by example by demonstrating a commitment to diversity

- Develop workplace policies, that support workplace diversity
- Promote diversity success stories
- Assist staff in balancing their work and personal lives.

V. Diversity Strategies

A. Awareness
- The organization is committed to increasing the awareness and understanding of workplace diversity by:
  - Providing diversity training to all organizational members
  - Developing a diversity profile of the organization and sharing it with employees and the community
  - Providing ongoing information that targets workplace diversity
  - Integrating diversity into organizational publications, advertisements and news releases.

B. Work Practices
- The organization will implement work policies, systems and practices that support and promote workplace diversity such as:
  - Distributing a Code of Conduct to all employees that details the organization's commitment to workplace diversity
  - Implementing a workplace tolerance program that supports the rights of all employees
  - Maintaining employment equity by ensuring that the organization is an equal opportunity employer
  - Reviewing recruitment policies and practices to ensure there are no diversity barriers
  - Implementing a problem-solving procedure that allows individuals to voice their concerns and complaints about workplace inequities
  - Providing education and development opportunities to all employees to assist them in achieving their maximum potential.

C. Monitoring and Evaluation
- Data collection and analysis will be used to monitor and evaluate our diversity efforts by:
  - Conducting an annual diversity survey
  - Developing a cultural diversity profile that delineates the organization's focus on workplace diversity
  - Developing a diversity scorecard to track the organization's progress

- Benchmarking the organization against similar organizations to determine opportunities for improvement
- Conducting an annual audit of all workplace policies, practices and procedures.

D. Implementation
- The organization will implement a comprehensive workplace diversity program that will focus on the uniqueness and cultural diversity of the organization by:
  - Selecting an individual to coordinate the diversity strategies for the organization
  - Involving all members of the executive leadership team in implementing the workplace strategic plan
  - Training all organizational members about the workplace strategic plan
  - Communicating to all key stakeholders the strategies that have been identified to appropriately address workplace diversity
  - Identifying timelines, resources and expectations regarding implementing diversity strategies.

E. Organizational Actions
- The organization is driven to act on the diversity needs of the organization by:
  - Committing the financial and people resources needed to ensure diversity is a top priority for organization
  - Enlisting the support and involvement of all individuals in leadership positions
  - Soliciting feedback from employees and other key stakeholders regarding what is needed to ensure the organization remains committed to workplace diversity
  - Creating an organization which values all individuals
  - Supporting our employees by offering programs that help balance work and personal lives
  - Resolving employee concerns regarding diversity in a timely and appropriate manner.

Appendix B
Sample Code of Conduct

A Statement of Basic Values
XYZ Corp. recognizes its responsibilities to our customers, employees and the community we serve. Every member of XYZ Corp. must be committed to act in accordance with the values and principles supported by the organization. As an organization, we are committed to and support the following values:

- **Teamwork**
  - We pledge to support each other and value each other's opinions as we work to accomplish our stated goals.
- **Diversity**
  - We are committed to a diverse and equal access workplace. As a diverse workplace, we value all individuals as equal partners in our success.
- **Integrity**
  - We pledge to be truthful and honest in all of our interactions.
- **Innovation**
  - We encourage new ideas and creativity from all members of the organization.
- **Accountability**
  - We will take equal responsibility for our work results.
- **Service Excellence**
  - We are committed to providing superior service to our internal and external customers.
- **Compassionate and Caring Spirit**
  - We believe in treating everyone with compassion, respect and consideration.
- **Personal Fulfillment**
  - We value a working environment that fosters growth, pride, harmony, fun and mutual respect.

Diversity Statement
XYZ Corp. recognizes that all employees, regardless of job classification, ethnic background, race, color, gender, age, religion, disability or other diverse characteristics, are part of a knowledgeable and skilled work team that contributes equally to the success of the organization. We want to create a nurturing and accepting environment that values the uniqueness of all individuals. XYZ Corp. is also committed to an environment that is free from all forms of discrimination

and prejudice. We believe employees should have equal access to all of the benefits of the organization without fear of reprisals or personal rejections. As such, the organization and its members pledge to do the following to protect and foster a richly diverse work environment:

- We pledge to be honest and forthright in all of our workplace interactions.
- We pledge to maintain a working environment free of harassment of any kind.
- We pledge to show proper respect and consideration for one another at all times.
- We pledge to exercise tact and diplomacy toward everyone at all times.
- We pledge to respect the ethnic and religious backgrounds of all organizational members.
- We pledge to support equal employment opportunity with hiring, advancement and compensation based on merit and without regard to race, color, religion, gender, national origin, age, disability or other diverse characteristic.
- We pledge to provide training in diversity to all organizational members.
- We pledge to perform work duties in accordance with professional and legal standards.
- We pledge to maintain objectivity in the performance of our work duties and when interacting with internal and external customers.
- We pledge to provide an objective problem solving procedure to resolve differences of opinions.
- We pledge to appropriately address and report any perceived or actual violations of this Code of Conduct.
- We pledge as an organization to value workplace diversity as an integral part of the organization's culture.

Authorization of Receipt of Code of Conduct Statement:

I acknowledge receipt of XYZ Corp.'s Code of Conduct. I pledge to support the values and the components delineated in the organization's "Diversity Statement." I also agree to report any violations of the Code of Conduct to management or to the Human Resources Department.

Signature: _____

Please Print Name: _____

Department: _____

Date: _____

Note: Some elements used in this example were adapted from Trover Foundation's Code of Conduct.

Appendix C
Sample Policy and Procedure

Magna Corp. Sample Policy and Procedure

Number: 1

Policy: Job Sharing
Approved by: Vice President—Human Resources

Original Date: August 8, (Year)	Date Last Reviewed/Revised: March 1, (Year)	Effective Date: March 1, (Year)

References: Policy on Worksharing

Policy and Scope
It is a policy of Magna Corp. to provide employees with an option to share an approved position as dictated by workloads and organizational needs. Job sharing will be approved on an individual basis and within the scope of prudent staffing needs.

Purpose
To provide flexible work arrangements to meet the needs of the employee and the organization.

Definitions
Job sharing is a staffing arrangement that allows two or more people to share a full-time equivalent position.

Procedure

A. **Voluntary Worksharing**

1. A job-share register has been established to place employees in positions approved for job sharing.
2. The job-share register will ensure that all interested employees meet the qualifications established for the position.
3. Employees interested in job sharing must submit a formal request to the Human Resources Department.
4. The departmental manager will then review and approve all job-share requests.
5. If approved for a job-sharing opportunity, the involved employees must meet with the manager to determine how to formalize the job-share arrangement.
6. The employees involved in the job-share arrangement are primarily responsible for ensuring the appropriate staffing for the shared position.
7. All parties involved in the job-sharing arrangement must ensure there is a "seamless" transition between work shifts, schedules and assigned tasks.
8. All employees involved in the job share are equally accountable for performing the full-time job within established performance standards.
9. Depending on the work schedule, an individual employee may not be eligible for certain total rewards programs or may be eligible on a prorated basis. The Human Resources Department will meet to discuss eligibility for total rewards programs.
10. Employees leaving a job-sharing arrangement must provide at least a two-week notice to their supervisor and to the Human Resources Department.

Magna Corp. Sample Policy and Procedure (Continued)

Text/References

Study on Flexible Work Schedules conducted by the Alliance for Work-Life Progress and The Regional Research Institute for Human Services

P&P Hospitalwide General Typing Instructions

1. Type Font Times New Roman
2. Title Times New Roman Size 12
3. Title box Times New Roman Size 10
4. Body of policy: Size 10
5. 1-inch margins
6. Page 1 of 1, etc. on bottom of each page.
7. Header with title of document on top of each page
8. If no number, move title box up to save space
9. File name: Optional, size 8
10. If you do not need a specific heading, delete it.

Magna Corp. Sample Policy and Procedure

Number: 2

Policy: Worksharing
Approved by: Vice President—Human Resources

Original Date: August 8, (Year)	Date Last Reviewed/Revised: March 1, (Year)	Effective Date: March 1, (Year)

Policy and Scope

When workloads are low, employees will be asked to work in other areas or jobs in the organization, in which they normally may not work. Employees will either be reassigned to other jobs or shifts where there is a staffing need or asked to engage in "worksharing" with other departments or units. The employee may volunteer to "share work" in other areas when staffing levels are low. If employees do not volunteer to work in other areas or jobs, they may be asked to go home without pay. Below is the procedure for instituting work sharing.

Purpose

Magna Corp. recognizes that all employees, regardless of job classification, possess unique skills and knowledge that contribute to the success of the organization. Magna Corp. wants to create a nurturing and positive environment in which employees are treated fairly and have ample opportunity.

Definitions

Worksharing is temporarily working in another job or work area. Worksharing may be either voluntary or mandatory, depending on staffing needs.

Procedure

A. Voluntary Worksharing

1. The Department Director or designee asks for volunteers to work other jobs or go to other work areas having a staffing need.

2. Employees must be qualified or willing to be trained to work in the area or job in which they volunteer.

3. Requests for voluntary worksharing are approved based on the following priority:

    a. Staffing needs — If the employee is needed in his or her regular job or work area, he or she may be denied his or her request to work other jobs or in other work areas. Work volumes and staffing needs are primary considerations in approving requests for voluntary worksharing. Volunteering to work in other areas will be noted on the employee's performance evaluation. Those who display a willingness to volunteer will be asked first if they want to voluntarily workshare.

Magna Corp. Sample Policy and Procedure (Continued)

  b. Amount of recent overtime — Employees will normally be sent home rather than paying overtime to work in other areas of the organization.

  c. Duration of assignment — If the employee is going to engage in worksharing on an ongoing basis (i.e., longer than four weeks), it may be necessary to reassign that employee on an equal basis to that job, shift or work area. At that time the employee's salary may be adjusted up or down if the job is at a different pay grade level.

  d. Amount of voluntary worksharing already granted — Employees would have an equal opportunity to volunteer for worksharing if skills are equal.

4. Voluntary worksharing can be approved for part of a work shift based on staffing needs.

B. Mandatory Worksharing

1. Mandatory worksharing will be implemented when employees do not volunteer to work in areas needing additional staff.

2. Employees will be reassigned to areas needing additional staff based on the following guidelines:

  a. Staffing Needs — Mandatory worksharing will be implemented first in those areas having a critical staffing need.

  b. Skills and Qualifications — The employee must possess the skills, qualifications, and willingness to be trained to do the work in the job or area.

  c. Amount of worked time — Employees normally will not be asked to work in another area or job if it means paying overtime.

3. Employees who refuse a mandatory workshare will be sent home without pay.

  a. Employees who report to work and are asked to go home because of "lack of work" will be paid at least one hour of compensation. Every effort will be made to place employees in another assignment before sending them home. Employees refusing a mandatory workshare will not be paid one hour of compensation for reporting to work.

  b. Employees may be placed on other shifts based on work volumes.

  c. Mandatory work sharing can be instituted for part of a work shift based on staffing needs.

Appendix D
Sample Cultural Survey

Sample Cultural Survey

Magna Corp. is conducting a survey about the workplace culture and environment. Your opinion will be used to evaluate cultural practices and values.

All responses are confidential.

The statements in the survey below should be answered by circling a number (e.g., 1, 2, 3, 4 or 5) which comes closest to your opinion about the statement:

Scale: 1 = Strongly Disagree

2 = Disagree

3 = Neutral (Neither Agree nor Disagree)

4 = Agree

5 = Strongly Agree

Thank you for your participation in the survey.

I. Culture and Personal Values

1. The organization's cultural goals have been communicated to me.

    1   2   3   4   5

2. I feel comfortable that my personal values will not be compromised by the organization.

    1   2   3   4   5

3. The organization's culture matches my personal beliefs and values.

    1   2   3   4   5

4. I understand and support the cultural goals of the organization.

    1   2   3   4   5

5. The organization is committed to helping the employee balance his or her home life with work.

    1   2   3   4   5

II. Cultural Diversity

6. The organization treats all individuals with dignity and respect regardless of their gender, disability, race, ethnic background or other unique characteristics.

    1   2   3   4   5

7. The organization provides a diversity training to all employees.

    1   2   3   4   5

8. The organization is committed to providing all employees with equal opportunities in the workplace.

    1   2   3   4   5

Sample Cultural Survey (Continued)

9. I understand and support the organization's diversity goals.

    1 2 3 4 5

10. The organization has a zero tolerance for any harassment in the workplace.

    1 2 3 4 5

III. Environment

11. The organization is fair and does not favor one employee over another in applying rules and policies.

    1 2 3 4 5

12. Employees are provided honest and open communication from the organization about important issues and changes.

    1 2 3 4 5

13. I feel comfortable reporting to my supervisor anyone I witness harassing or mistreating a co-worker or customer.

    1 2 3 4 5

14. Job promotions and transfer opportunities are objective and impartial.

    1 2 3 4 5

15. I believe the organization's practices, policies and procedures are administered objectively and consistently.

    1 2 3 4 5

IV. Job Satisfaction and Workplace Value

16. I feel valued by the organization for my work contributions.

    1 2 3 4 5

17. I am well satisfied with my job.

    1 2 3 4 5

18. The organization encourages cooperation and teamwork.

    1 2 3 4 5

19. I believe the organization has a reputation in the community for valuing its employees.

    1 2 3 4 5

20. The organizational culture and work environment contribute positively to the overall employee morale.

    1 2 3 4 5

21. Please provide any additional feedback about the organization's culture or work environment:_____

    _____

Appendix E
Policy Audit

Policy Audit	
Policy/Practice: _____	**Effective Date:** _____

I. General Audit

Category/Question	Y/N	General Description

1. Does the practice/policy identify who is responsible for administering it? Identify person or department responsibilities in the General Description.

2. Is there a general policy or practice? If so, discuss in the General Description.

3. Is there a stated purpose for the policy or practice? If so, discuss in the General Description.

4. Does the policy/practice identify who is covered or eligible? List who is covered by the policy in the General Description.

5. Does the policy/practice include a general definition of how it is to be administered? If so, please discuss in the General Description.

6. Does the policy/practice have a step-by-step procedure that provides guidelines for interpreting and administering it? If yes, list at least two procedures/guidelines in the General Description.

7. Has the policy been reviewed or revised in the past 12 months? List review/revision date(s) in the General Description.

8. Are there any implications or sanctions listed in the policy/practice for failing to comply with it? If yes, list the implications or sanctions in the General Description.

9. Does the policy/practice use language that clearly explains its intent? Please elaborate in the General Description.

10. Are there monitors in place to determine compliance with the policy/practice? If yes, list some of the monitors in the General Description.

II. General Review and Recommendation

Please answer the following questions:

1. What areas are not covered by the policy/practice?

2. What are your recommendations for improving the policy/practice?

3. How would you communicate this policy/practice to employees? Managers? Customers?

4. What implications, if any, does this policy or practice have on work-life strategies?

5. What implications, if any, does this policy or practice have on cultural diversity?

Appendix F
Sample Talking Points for Cultural Diversity Program

WHAT?
- The organization will be conducting diversity training with all employees.
- An extensive diversity audit will be conducted with all employees and leaders to determine how the organization is doing regarding diversity.
- From the audit and feedback from other key stakeholders, a strategic plan focused solely on diversity will be developed and implemented.
- Focus groups comprised of randomly selected employees will be conducted to solicit input about diversity and how it impacts the work environment.
- An audit of all policies and practices will be conducted to ensure diversity and equal opportunity are appropriately incorporated.
- A cultural survey will be administered to all employees to solicit feedback about the organization's culture and its impact on work life.
- The organization will review the impact and appropriateness of all total rewards programs on cultural diversity.
- A cross-functional team comprised of key stakeholders and managers will review work-life strategies and make recommendations to the organization regarding new programs and approaches that will help the employee balance work with his or her personal life.

WHY?
- The organization seeks to raise the employee awareness about cultural diversity.
- It is important to the organization to create a positive culture and work environment.
- All of these programs and strategies are being done to develop a culture that values all individuals equally.
- The audit is being conducted to ensure that the organization's policies and practices safeguard all individuals.
- The organization seeks to provide work-life strategies that will assist the organization in recruiting and retaining qualified employees.

HOW?
- Each department will develop and communicate to its employees its plan to promote cultural diversity.

- Results of the cultural survey will be communicated to all key stakeholders by direct mail and on the organization's Web site.
- A randomly selected group of employees will be asked to participate in focus groups.
- "Talking points" for specific issues regarding diversity will be provided to managers to communicate a consistent message to employees.
- The organization will communicate to employees progress made on work-life strategies and other viable diversity issues via the following methods:
  - Intranet
  - Letter from the CEO sent personally to each employee
  - Departmental meetings
  - Payroll stuffers
  - Open forums with employees
- Housewide training on diversity will be offered during a four-week period via live and video recorded presentations.
- Policy and practice audits will be conducted by a cross-functional team with oversight by an outside firm that specializes in diversity management.

WHO?
- Senior leadership and department directors are responsible for developing a communication plan for their work areas.
- All employees will be asked to voluntarily participate in the cultural survey.
- Focus group participants will be selected from a variety of job titles.
- All members of management are encouraged to provide feedback about diversity issues in their work areas.
- All employees will receive diversity training during a four-week period.
- An outside consulting firm will be used to assist in auditing the organization's policies and practices.

WHEN?
- Focus groups will be conducted during a three-week period beginning April 1, (Year).
- The cultural survey will be administered June 1 through June 30, (Year).
- The policy and practice audit will be Aug. 1, (Year).
- A strategy plan about diversity will be submitted to the board of directors for approval no later than Nov. 1, (Year).
- The diversity training program will be conducted housewide Jan. 10 to Feb. 7, (Year).

Appendix G
Sample Communication Plan

Sample Communication Plan				
Step(s)	**Action(s)**	**Expected Outcome(s)**	**Resources**	**Timetable**
1. Initial employee meetings	Conduct meetings with employees at the departmental level to discuss diversity and cultural issues.	Solicit feedback from employees regarding cultural and diversity concerns.	• Employees • Managers • Senior leadership	14 – 21 days
2. Employee focus groups	Conduct focus groups with a randomly selected group of employees.	Objective feedback about diversity and work-life needs.	• Facilitator • Diversity consultant as needed • Employees	7 – 14 days
3. Survey feedback	Provide feedback to employees about the cultural survey.	Verify the data collected from employees who participated in the cultural survey.	• Employees • Key stakeholders • Senior leadership • HR representative • Outside consultants as needed	14 – 21 days
4. Audit feedback	Provide feedback to employees and key stakeholders about the policy audit and what actions, if any, will be forthcoming.	Provide employees and key stakeholders information about how the policies and practices of the organization integrate with the culture.	• Key stakeholders • Employees • HR representative • Outside consultant as needed • Legal counsel	14 – 21 days
5. Work-life strategy team	Identify and recommend work-life strategies to senior leadership.	Ensure organization is addressing the work-life needs of its employees.	• Work-life strategy team • HR staff • Key stakeholders • Employees • Senior leadership • Outside consultants as needed	21 – 28 days
6. Announcement of diversity strategy	The CEO will send a letter to the employee's home announcing the organization's strategy on diversity.	Promote diversity as an important element of the organization's work environment.	• CEO • Employees • Key stakeholders • Board • Legal counsel • Outside consultants as necessary	10 – 14 days

Sample Communication Plan (Continued)

Step(s)	Action(s)	Expected Outcome(s)	Resources	Timetable
7. Announcement of new diversity training program	Inform employees of a new training program that will focus solely on diversity. The announcement will be sent to the employee's home and posted on the organization's Web site.	Generate excitement and support for the training program.	• CEO • Senior leadership • Employees • Key stakeholders • HR staff • Outside consultants if needed	10 – 14 days
8. Diversity training	Conduct diversity training with all employees and key stakeholders.	Increase awareness of diversity and its importance in the workplace.	• Employees • Key stakeholders • Diversity Coordinator if designated • Trainers • HR staff • Outside diversity training sources as needed	28 – 35 days

9. Ongoing communication	Provide ongoing communication about diversity and work-life strategies.	Communicate to employees any new strategies and approaches concerning diversity and work-life issues as they are developed.	• CEO
			• Employees
			• Key stakeholders
			• Senior leadership
			• HR staff
			  - Diversity Coordinator if designated
			  - Intranet
			  - Departmental meetings
			  - Informational forums
			  - Written communication
				Ongoing

Appendix H
Flexible Work Schedules

Survey Brief

WorldatWork, the Alliance for Work-Life Progress and the Regional Research Institute for Human Services at Portland State University

October 2005

Introduction & Methodology

In August 2005, WorldatWork, The Alliance for Work-Life Progress (AWLP) and The Regional Research Institute for Human Services at Portland State University conducted a survey to identify trends in work-life policies and practices. Survey participants were asked about the prevalence and use of flexible work arrangements, as well as their level of knowledge about various work-life and dependent-care issues.

For the purposes of this survey, "flexible work arrangements" refer to choices about the time and/or location that work is conducted (Rau, 2003)[1]. For example, altering starting and quitting times or working from home are both considered flexible work arrangements. Here, a "formal" flexible work arrangement is written into organizational policy and the employee and supervisor must follow organizational procedure, while "informal" flexible arrangements are based on supervisory discretion and can be undocumented (Eaton, 2003)[2]

Surveys were emailed to 4,645 WorldatWork and AWLP members, and 552 participants completed the survey. Results of individual questions are presented in the "Detailed Survey Results" section. Please note that totals may not always equal 100 percent due to rounding differences.

Executive Summary

Flexible work schedules and work-life supports create opportunities for both employees and employers. Employers appreciate the boost in productivity and morale while employees reap the benefits of structuring work around their lives instead of the other way around. Although flexible work scheduling can be a win-win situation under the right circumstances, it goes against the traditional Western work culture. In the United States specifically, the customary work ethic has always boasted long hours and face time at the office as essential ingredients of the recipe to success. How much has the modern Western work culture welcomed flexibility as a viable business strategy and how far do we still have to go?

While results of this study indicate workplace cultures in the United States are trying to incorporate flexibility and enhance work-life integration for some employees with particular needs, there are more steps to take before flexible schedules evolve beyond isolated, individual perks. Employees who disclose a personal reason for a flexible work request are more likely to have it approved in three out of four organizations, although something more than "I would like more control over my schedule" appears necessary. Requests due to medical, child care or other urgent personal matters are likely to be approved, perhaps because a "good enough reason" is required to trump the traditional presumption about when, where and how we work.

A mounting awareness of the need for work-life balance is beginning to erode the traditional business adage that counseled employees to leave their personal lives at home. More than half of participants regard their organizational cultures as receptive to handling personal issues on company time, although 40 percent say the attitude is highly dependent on individual supervisors, suggesting the potential for multiple cultures to exist in one workplace. For organizations to fully capitalize on the benefits of flexible work, employees will need visible acknowledgement and encouragement from organization leaders.

Other highlights of the survey include:

- Nine in 10 organizations participating in this survey offer a flexible scheduling program, and more than half of flexibility programs operate informally. Forty-four percent have a formal policy, while about 5 percent do not have a flexible work program.
- About one in three participants maintain their work culture does not encourage employees to work flexible schedules, even though they are offered.
- The most common way for employees to request a flexible work arrangement in nine out of 10 organizations is to verbally contact the immediate supervisor.
- What factors are most important to employers when considering a flexible work request? Most frequently, employers weigh the impact on coverage, the ability of the employee to complete their duties, and the impact on customers most heavily when deciding whether or not to grant a flexible work request.

Detailed Survey Results

Flexible work arrangements operate on an informal basis in more than 50 percent of organizations, although only 44 percent have implemented formal policies and procedures (See Figure 1.) Only about 5 percent do not have either type of policy.

Formal flexible work policies are fairly new to most organizations. About one in four organizations created their programs in the last five years, and another 16 percent added them in the last six to 10 years. (See Figure 2.) Only about 7 percent of policies have aged more than 10 years, and a full 45 percent still have no formal policies regarding flexible work.

Which employees are eligible for flexible work schedules? Salaried employees have the widest array of flexible arrangements at their disposal, at least on an informal basis. (See Figure 3.) About half of the organizations surveyed report their salaried employees can exercise flextime on a daily basis, and slightly more than half can telecommute. Hourly employees have somewhat more restricted access to flexible work. About one in three organizations offer flextime to hourly employees, including daily flextime, on an informal basis. Telework, defined as working from home on a full-time basis and rarely visiting the worksite, is not available for any employees at

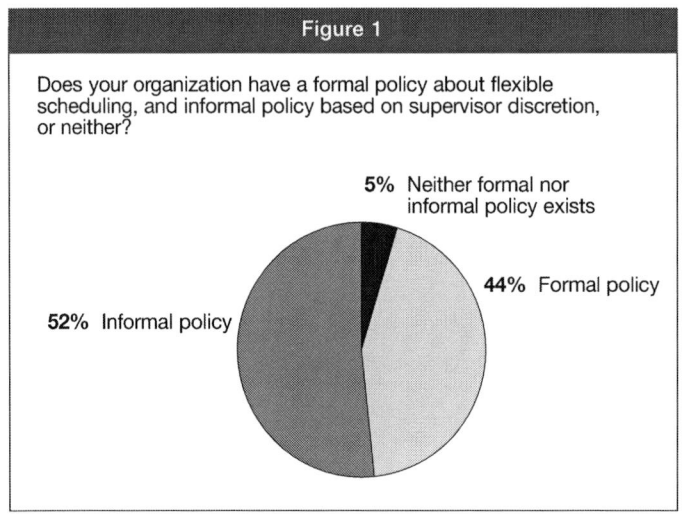

Figure 1

Does your organization have a formal policy about flexible scheduling, and informal policy based on supervisor discretion, or neither?

- 5% Neither formal nor informal policy exists
- 44% Formal policy
- 52% Informal policy

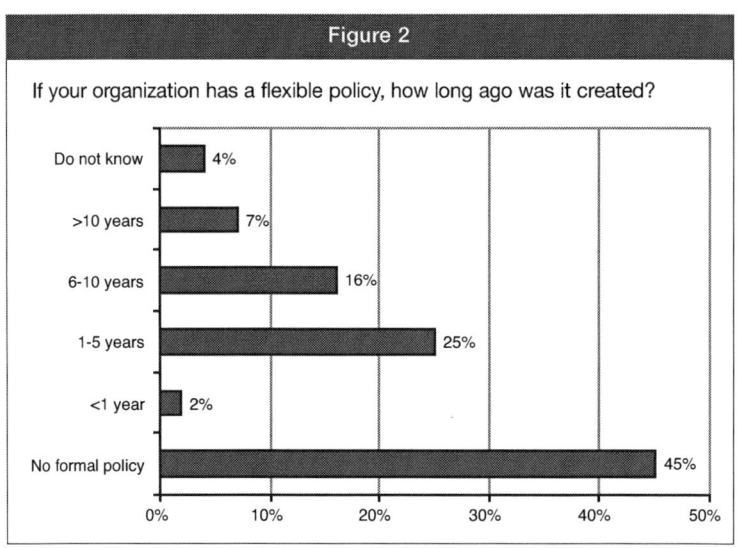

Figure 2

If your organization has a flexible policy, how long ago was it created?

- Do not know: 4%
- >10 years: 7%
- 6-10 years: 16%
- 1-5 years: 25%
- <1 year: 2%
- No formal policy: 45%

a majority (60 percent) of organizations. Employees also lack access to job sharing either formally or informally in 60 percent of the organizations surveyed.

Although salaried employees have an edge in exercising flexible work schedules, a majority of organizations make flexible benefits available to different types of employees. (See Figure 4.) Eight in 10 employers offer flexible arrangements to professional employees. Clerical/administrative, technical and managerial employees can access flexible work arrangements in three out of four organizations. Asking whether flexible arrangements are accessible and whether more than 50 percent of employees in the category exercise flexible scheduling are two different questions. Indeed, access is more typical than majority practice. (See Figure 4.) Only a small percentage of employers report that flexible schedules are used by more than 50 percent of employees in each category. For example, 15 percent of organizations report that more than 50 percent of their professional employees actually flex their schedules.

Figure 3

Which of the following flexible work arrangements is available in your organization? (Respondent checked all that applied.)[3]

	Salaried		Hourly		Not Available
	Formal	Informal	Formal	Informal	
Flextime	37%	49%	29%	31%	15%
Daily Flextime	13%	53%	8%	30%	33%
Compressed workweek	24%	23%	23%	16%	46%
Telecommute	28%	54%	15%	19%	19%
Telework	18%	16%	9%	6%	60%
Part-time work schedules	36%	27%	32%	20%	28%
Job Share	19%	10%	14%	9%	61%

Figure 4

Which of the following types of employees have access to and/or use flexible work arrangements in your organization? (Respondent checked all that applied.)

	Accessible	Used by more than 50% of employees	Not applicable
Clerical/Administrative	73%	13%	19%
Technical	74%	14%	16%
Professional	84%	15%	10%
Managerial	78%	14%	14%
Sales/Customer Service	54%	11%	28%

Flexible work arrangements may be accessible, but workplace culture can play a huge role in determining whether or not employees actually make use of the opportunity. About 56 percent of organizations report their culture is supportive of employees taking time at work for personal issues, although a sizable minority (40 percent) say the level of support is highly dependent on individual supervisors. (See Figure 5.) Given the potential number of departments, a schism within organizations may exist where some employees feel flexibility and work-life supports are acceptable while others believe the practices are frowned upon. Only 5 percent acknowledge that their organizations do not support employees taking time at work for routine personal or family issues.

Although flexible work arrangements exist within a majority of organizations, employees may not feel free to utilize the option. Employees may perceive a gap between the offer of flexibility and the acceptability of actually practicing it. About one in three HR professionals report that their cultures do not encourage the use of flexible work arrangements. (See Figure 6.)

Supervisors play an important role in arranging flexible schedules. As depicted in Figure 7, almost 90 percent of survey respondents cite contacting the immediate supervisor as the most common way to plan a flexible schedule. Less than half ask employees to e-mail their direct supervisors, and 36 percent request employees verbally contact human resources.

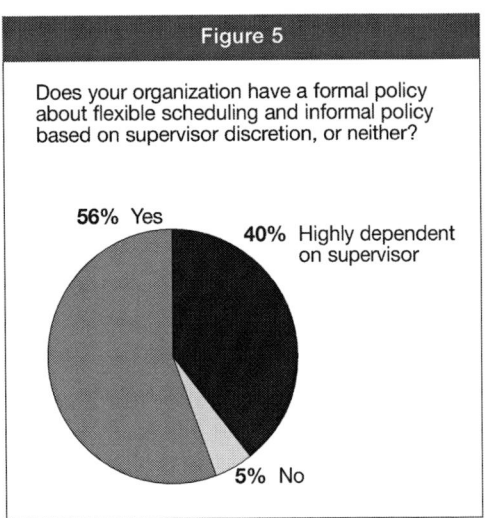

Figure 5

Does your organization have a formal policy about flexible scheduling and informal policy based on supervisor discretion, or neither?

56% Yes
40% Highly dependent on supervisor
5% No

Figure 6	
From your perspective, what is the primary reason employees do not use flexible work arrangements?	
Even though the organization offers them, the culture doesn't encourage the use of flexible work arrangements	34%
Flexible work arrangements do not meet employee needs	11%
Employees do not know about flexible work arrangements	5%
Do not know	13%
Not Applicable	19%
Other	18%

Establishing policies and practices related to flexible work resides with HR departments in the majority of organizations surveyed. (See Figure 8.) While HR professionals may be responsible for formal policies and practices, many flexible programs operate on an informal level, with supervisors approving and implementing the schedules. About one in three respondents indicate that their flexible work program is decentralized, with decisions made at the line or supervisor level.

Employees who discuss why they need a flexible schedule increase the likelihood of securing approval for the request in three out of four organizations. (See Figure 9.) Flexible scheduling may not be such an acceptable option that it can be secured automatically or without any particular reason, although about 15 percent of organizations indicated disclosure has no bearing on the decision. Nearly one in 10 do not want to hear the personal reasons behind the request out of concern for potential liability.

Flexible scheduling has practical implications for the employee and the employer. We asked participants how much weight they assign certain factors when evaluating a flexible work proposal. The results are shown in Figure 10. The most dominant considerations involved the employee's ability to meet job responsibilities, impact on coverage and impact on customers. The nature of the job duties was afforded significant weight in 78 percent of organizations. A majority also weighs employee's past performance and supervisor's recommendation heavily.

Disclosure of the personal reasons prompting a flexible work request helps many employees secure their employer's approval. Does disclosure of any reason make approval more likely, or are

Figure 7

Which of the following are ways employees can request flexible work arrangements? (Respondent checked all that applied.)

Verbally contact immediate supervisor	89%
E-mail direct supervisor	49%
Verbally contact HR	36%
E-mail the HR department	23%
Complete standardized paperwork	22%
Verbally contact coworkers	5%
File a request form online	5%
Verbally contact work-life department	4%
E-mail work-life department	3%

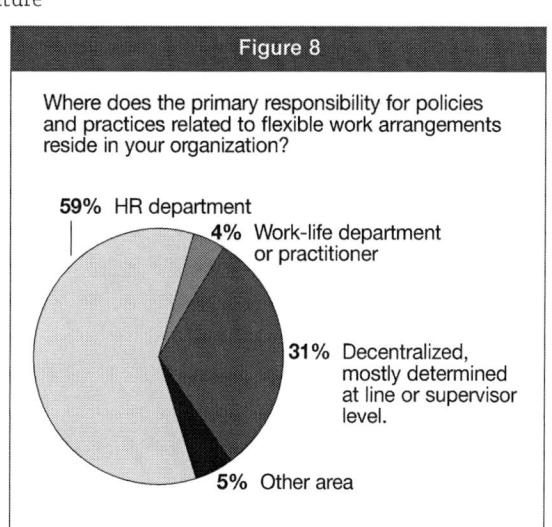

Figure 8

Where does the primary responsibility for policies and practices related to flexible work arrangements reside in your organization?

- 59% HR department
- 4% Work-life department or practitioner
- 31% Decentralized, mostly determined at line or supervisor level.
- 5% Other area

employers likely to respond more favorably to certain types of reasons than others? Survey participants were asked how likely they were to grant flexible work requests given a variety of different reasons. (See Figure 11.) Granting a flexible schedule request due to terminal illness of a family member was "very likely" to be approved in 56 percent of organizations, and short-term child-care difficulties would "likely" earn approval in 50 percent of organizations. Employees who ask to work flexible schedules so they can seek drug or alcohol treatment would "likely" be granted permission in eight out of 10 organizations, while asking for flexible work to support a family's members drug rehabilitation would "likely" receive approval in about six out of 10 workplaces.

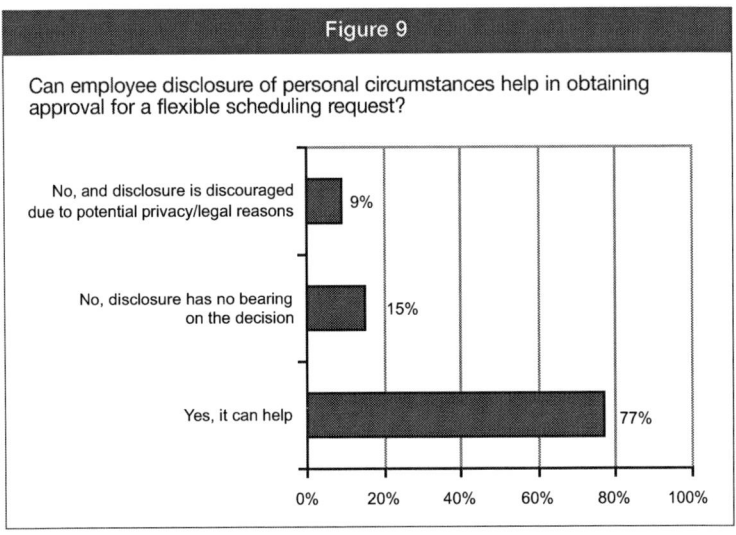

Figure 9

Can employee disclosure of personal circumstances help in obtaining approval for a flexible scheduling request?

- No, and disclosure is discouraged due to potential privacy/legal reasons: 9%
- No, disclosure has no bearing on the decision: 15%
- Yes, it can help: 77%

Figure 10

In your organization, how much weight is given to the following factors when the average employee's proposal for flexible work is being evaluated?

	Little weight	Some weight	Significant weight	Not applicable
Employee's ability to continue job responsibilities	<1%	6%	90%	4%
Impact on customers	<1%	8%	86%	5%
Impact on coverage	2%	9%	85%	4%
Employee's job duties	2%	17%	78%	3%
Supervisor's recommendation	3%	24%	68%	5%
Employee's past job performance	5%	30%	60%	5%
Length of time employee needs arrangement	12%	38%	43%	6%
Reason for request	12%	39%	41%	8%
Employee retention	12%	49%	34%	5%

Parents whose children are experiencing behavioral difficulties at school may find their employers somewhat ambivalent about granting a flexible work schedule on that justification. About 44 percent of employers were neither "likely" nor "unlikely" to grant a flexible schedule for a parent whose child was acting out at school and 43 percent were swayed in neither direction for a parent whose child was expelled from school. Employers were least likely to grant flexible schedules for employees training for a marathon — six in 10 participants said their organizations would be "unlikely" or "very unlikely" to grant such a request. Employers also would be less likely to approve a flexible schedule so an employee can care for a sick animal.

Flexible work schedules can make good business sense for an organization. A variety of outcomes can result from implementing a flexible work program, and survey participants were asked to anticipate how their leadership would weight

Figure 11

The following are some reasons employees give when requesting flexible work arrangements. Please rate how likely approval would be granted for each reason.

	Not likely at all	Unlikely	Neither likely nor unlikely	Likely	Very likely to grant request
Short-term child-care difficulties	2%	4%	13%	50%	32%
Short-term child illness	1%	1%	7%	40%	50%
Family member with health issues	<1%	1%	13%	45%	41%
Terminal illness of family member	<1%	<1%	9%	34%	56%
Ongoing chronic health condition of employee	<1%	2%	13%	40%	44%
Child with ongoing chronic health condition	<1%	2%	16%	43%	38%
Elderly parent needing care	<1%	5%	22%	47%	26%
Child acting out at school	4%	12%	44%	29%	11%
Training for a marathon	23%	35%	30%	9%	3%
Child therapy appointment	3%	4%	22%	46%	25%
Physical therapy for employee injury	2%	2%	11%	40%	46%
Child expelled from school	6%	13%	43%	25%	13%
Drug or alcohol treatment for self	2%	2%	15%	37%	44%
Drug or alcohol treatment for family	3%	7%	32%	39%	19%
Care for sick animal	20%	25%	36%	14%	5%
Child with disability needing care	1%	2%	18%	44%	35%
Mental health treatment for self	2%	2%	15%	38%	44%
Mental health treatment for family	3%	5%	26%	41%	26%
Self-development (courses, education, lessons)	5%	9%	33%	38%	15%

the significance of various business results. (See Figure 12.) Three out of four organizations said improving employee satisfaction would be given at least strong consideration, and 72 percent strongly value employee retention. More than half found increasing employee productivity persuasive. Given the effect of stress on productivity, it was surprising that 60 percent of employers perceived declining employee mental health as weak, or holding no weight one way or the other. Perception of fairness among employees also did not sway employers for, or against, implementing flexible work schedules.

Flexible work arrangements operate informally in a majority of organizations. An assumption that flexible work can be worked out on a case-by-case with individual supervisors may explain the lack of formal inquiry about employees' flexibility needs. If employee needs are handled at the line or supervisor level, a formal survey of employee needs may be identified as unnecessary and duplicative. As shown in Figure 13, 86 percent of organizations in this study do not regularly ask employees about their flexible scheduling needs.

Figure 12

From the perspective of your organizational leadership, how strong are the following business reasons for allowing employees to have flexible work schedules?

	Very weak	Weak	Neither strong nor weak	Strong	Very strong
Improves employee retention	3%	5%	21%	45%	27%
Improves employee productivity	4%	8%	31%	37%	21%
Improves employee job satisfaction	3%	3%	17%	52%	25%
Decreases employee stress	3%	8%	31%	42%	16%
Decreases employee mental health problems	3%	11%	46%	29%	10%
Improves employee commitment	2%	5%	22%	50%	22%
Improves quality of life for employees and families	2%	4%	21%	47%	26%
Improves recruitment of a diverse workforce	4%	11%	31%	36%	19%
Improves employee engagement	3%	7%	29%	44%	18%
Improves employee work-life balance	2%	5%	21%	46%	27%
Improves employee morale	2%	4%	18%	52%	25%
Decreases employee absenteeism	2%	7%	29%	45%	16%
Improves perception of fairness among all employees	4%	15%	42%	28%	10%
Increases the public image of being an employer of choice	5%	8%	30%	40%	17%
Increases social responsibility	6%	13%	42%	28%	11%

Where do HR professionals go to learn about their employees' dependent care needs? Figure 14 demonstrates that most often, they reach out to organizations that are familiar to them such as HR professional organizations (20 percent) and employee assistance providers (EAPs) (28 percent.) About 16 percent cite child and eldercare resource services as the best informants. Very few HR professionals turn to professional training or rely on personal experience, both of which were marked by less than 1 percent of participants.

HR professionals also feel fairly comfortable in their level of knowledge about various dependent-care issues. For example, three out of four survey respondents believe they are at least "knowledgeable" about parenting and 68 percent believe they are at least "knowledgeable" about child development from birth through age 12. (See Figure 15.) They report being less informed about child disabilities and mental health (38 percent each) and adult disabilities (39 percent).

Figure 13
Does your organization regularly survey employees about their work-family needs?

86% No
14% Yes

Figure 14
What is the single best resource for information regarding employees' dependent care issues? (Respondent checked one response only.)

EAPs	28%
HR professional organization	20%
Child and eldercare resource/referral service	16%
Colleagues	8%
Personal experience	5%
Parent/employee advisory group	3%
World Wide Web/Internet	3%
Continuing education	<1%
Professional training	<1%
Not applicable	10%

Figure 15
Please rate your personal level of knowledge about the following topics related to dependent care.

	Almost no knowledge	Not much knowledge	Neither knowledgeable	Somewhat knowledgeable	Very knowledgeable
Child development, birth-12	9%	10%	13%	44%	24%
Adolescent development, 13-21	10%	14%	21%	42%	13%
Parenting	7%	8%	12%	46%	28%
Eldercare responsibilities	6%	17%	19%	43%	15%
Adult disabilities	11%	21%	29%	33%	6%
Child disabilities	12%	22%	29%	33%	5%
Adult mental health	9%	18%	26%	40%	8%
Children's mental health	12%	22%	29%	33%	5%

Employees with questions about benefits are often directed to their HR department. Knowledge about local resources, especially as they relate to employee benefits, seems to be comfortable ground for survey participants. (See Figure 16.) Eight in 10 respondents state they are "familiar" or "very familiar" with health-care resources, 63 percent with child care, and 61 percent with employee stress management resources. Respondents felt least familiar with child mental health- care options (43 percent), eldercare (47 percent) and work-life integration (49 percent.)

High perceptions of comfort with dependent care and flexible scheduling needs may account for the relative lack of training that is offered to managers or supervisors. As shown in Figure 17, 81 percent of organizations have not offered training about flexible work arrangements for HR professionals in the last two years,

Figure 16

Please rate your level of familiarity with resources in your community addressing the following work-life issues of employees.

	Very unfamiliar	Unfamiliar	Neither Familiar or unfamiliar	Familiar	Very Familiar
Employee stress management	5%	12%	22%	48%	13%
Child care	4%	13%	20%	47%	16%
Parenting	4%	15%	26%	43%	12%
Work-life integration	5%	15%	30%	37%	12%
Health care	2%	6%	11%	48%	33%
Adult mental health care	5%	17%	25%	41%	12%
Drug and alcohol treatment	5%	15%	25%	43%	12%
Children's mental health care	6%	21%	29%	35%	8%
Eldercare	6%	17%	30%	35%	12%

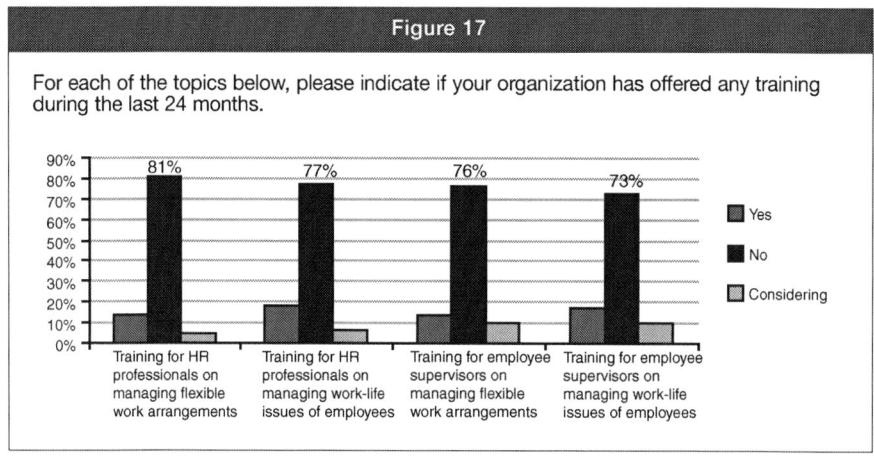

Figure 17

For each of the topics below, please indicate if your organization has offered any training during the last 24 months.

- Training for HR professionals on managing flexible work arrangements: 81% No
- Training for HR professionals on managing work-life issues of employees: 77% No
- Training for employee supervisors on managing flexible work arrangements: 76% No
- Training for employee supervisors on managing work-life issues of employees: 73% No

Legend: Yes / No / Considering

and three out of four have not trained HR employees on work-life issues. Supervisors have not been offered training about flexible scheduling or work-life matters in about three quarters of organizations surveyed.

To get a sense of the workplace culture regarding dependent-care needs, participants were asked how much they agreed or disagreed with a series of statements reflecting attitudes toward personal issues. The results indicate that respondents believe their workplaces are fairly sympathetic to dependent-care needs and flexible work. For example, 84 percent of respondents reject that their organization has an "unwritten rule" forbidding employees to deal with personal issues at work. Another 75 percent dispute the statement that their organizations look unfavorably on employees who put family needs ahead of their job.

Figure 18

For each statement below, please indicate the extent to which you agree or disagree, when you think about your organization.

	Strongly disagree	Somewhat disagree	Agree somewhat	Strongly agree
There is an unwritten rule at my place of employment that you cannot take care of family needs on company time.	49%	35%	13%	3%
At my place of employment, employees who put their family or personal needs ahead of their job are not looked on favorably.	37%	38%	22%	4%
If you have a problem managing your work and family responsibilities, the attitude at my place of employment is, "You made your bed, now lie in it."	51%	34%	13%	2%
At my place of employment, employees have to choose between advancing in their jobs and devoting attention to their family or personal lives.	30%	40%	24%	7%
In this organization, parents are encouraged to take time off work to care for their children with ongoing health issues.	7%	31%	45%	17%
In this organization, employees are reluctant to ask for flexible work arrangements.	26%	36%	32%	7%
In this organization, it is OK for parents to receive phone calls at work regarding their children with ongoing emotional or behavioral challenges.	4%	8%	47%	41%
Supervisors in this organization are supportive of the needs of employees who have children with disabilities.	3%	8%	54%	35%
Coworkers in this organization are not supportive of parents of children with emotional or behavioral challenges.	36%	45%	16%	4%

Somewhat inconsistently, 39 percent also indicate that employees are reluctant to ask for flexible work arrangements. What accounts for this perceived hesitation? As shown in Figure 6, one in three participants believes employees do not exercise flexible scheduling because the culture ultimately does not support it.

It is possible that while organizations are theoretically amenable to flexible scheduling and other work-life supports, employees may be waiting on acknowledgement from organizational leadership of their genuine acceptability.

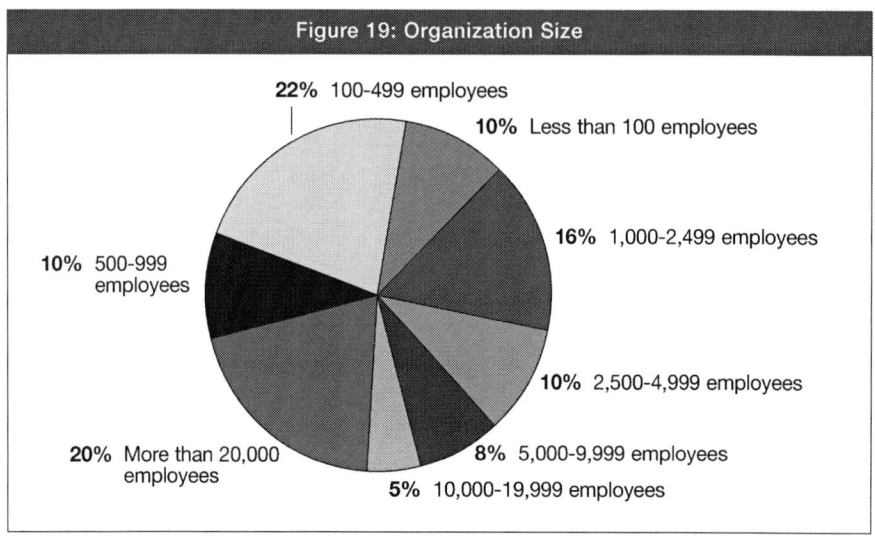

Figure 19: Organization Size

- 22% 100-499 employees
- 10% Less than 100 employees
- 16% 1,000-2,499 employees
- 10% 500-999 employees
- 10% 2,500-4,999 employees
- 20% More than 20,000 employees
- 8% 5,000-9,999 employees
- 5% 10,000-19,999 employees

Figure 20: Type of Industry

What is the single best resource for information regarding employees' dependent care issues? (Respondent checked one response only.)

Industry	%	Industry	%
Manufacturing	16%	Transportation and warehousing	2%
Finance and insurance	16%	Accommodation and food service	1%
Other	16%	Arts, entertainment and recreation	1%
Professional, scientific and technical	12%	Administrative support, waste and remediation	<1%
Health care and social assistance	6%	Agriculture	<1%
Information	6%	Construction	<1%
Other services (except public administration)	6%	Management of companies and enterprises	<1%
Utilities	5%	Mining	<1%
Public administration	4%	Real Estate, rental and leasing	<1%
Retail	4%	Wholesale Trade	<1%
Educational services	2%		

If key leaders do not openly vocalize their dedication to work-life integration and flexible scheduling, or practice it themselves, employees may remain reluctant to take the initiative.

Footnotes

1 Definition adapted from Rau, B. (2003). *Flexible work arrangements: A Sloan work and family encyclopedia entry.* Retrieved May 20, 2003, from http://wfnetwork.bc.edu/encyclopedia_template.php?id=240.

2 Formal v. Informal Definition taken from Eaton, S. (2003). If you can use them: Flexibility policies, organizational commitment, and perceived performance. *Industrial Relations*, 42 (2), 145-167.

3 Items adapted from the *Workplace Flexibility Index*. Bond, J.T., Thompson, C., Galinsky, E., & Prottas, D. (2003). Highlights of the National Study of the Changing Workforce. New York: Families & Work Institute.

Selected References

Bello, David C; Barnes, Summer. 2006. "The Sales-Incentive Entitlement Culture." *workspan*, August, 40-44.

Boglarsky, Cheryl A. 2005. "5 Steps to Successful Mergers & Acquisitions." *workspan*, February, 49-52.

Gilles, Paul. 2001. "Building a Foundation for Effective Pay Programs." *workspan*, September, 28-32.

Gilles, Paul. 2000. "The Importance of HR in Making Your Merger Work." *workspan*, August, 16-20.

Gostick, Adrian. 2003. "A Hero's Welcome: Improving Culture with Noncash Rewards and Recognition." *workspan*, July, 44-47.

Fineman, Michal. 2004. "Get the Most out of Assessing Your Work Environment." *workspan*, May, 42-46.

Heher, Eliot C. 2006. "Anticipating the Psychological Effects of Expatriate Life." *workspan*, May, 55-56.

Jones, Keith D. 2005. "The Culture Quandary: Creating An Organizational Fit." *workspan*, October, 12-13.

Kadilak, Kathryn O.; Watts, Diana. 2006. "Revisiting the Work-Life Dialogue." *workspan*, May, 38-42.

Morgan, Robert. 2004. "Retention Report Card: Does Your Organization Make the Grade?" *workspan*, February, 18-20.

O'Neal, Sandra. 2005. "Total Rewards and the Future of Work." *workspan*, January, 18-26.

Parus, Barbara. 2004. "Pump Up Your Flexibility Quotient." *workspan*, August, 47-53.

Parus, Barbara. 2003. "Workplace Stress: How Do Employees Get Relief?" *workspan*, June, 40-43.

Parus, Barbara. 2002. "Effective Rewards Support Culture Change." *workspan*, November, 20-23.

Polack, Richard. 2006. "Culture in a Box: The Ten Steps of a Successful Company." *workspan*, February, 8-9.

Schinnerer, John. 2003. "The ROI of an Effective Ethics Program." *workspan*, October, 52-55.

Wellins, Richard; Rioux, Sheila. 2001. "Solving the Global HR Puzzle." *workspan*, February, 26-29.

WorldatWork Surveys (www.worldatwork.org/library/research/ surveys)

2006 State of the Work-Life Profession

2005 Flexible Work Schedules

2005 Trends in Employee Recognition

2005 State of Work-Life Profession

2003 – Recognition

2002 Practices in the Work Experience

2002 Retention Bonus Survey

2002 Spot Bonus Survey

WorldatWork Bookstore (www.worldatwork.org/bookstore)

Baryon, G. Michael. 2002. *Recognition at Work*. Scottsdale: WorldatWork Press.

Bellingham, Richard. 2001. *The Manager's Pocket Guide to Corporate Culture Change*. Amherst: HRD Press.

Gallagher, Richard S. 2003. *The Soul of an Organization: Understanding the Values that Drive Successful Corporate Cultures*. Chicago: Dearborn Trade Publishing.

Harris, Philip R.; Moran, Robert T.; Moran, Sarah V. 2004. *Managing Cultural Difference: Global Leadership Strategies for the Twenty-first Century*. St. Louis: Elsevier Butterworth-Heinemann.

Horibe, Frances. 2001. *Creating the Innovation Culture: Leveraging Visionaries, Dissenters and Other Useful Troublemakers in Your Organization*. San Francisco: John Wiley & Sons.

Corey Rosen, Corey; Carberry, Ed. 2002. *Ownership Management: Building a Culture of Lasting Innovation*. Oakland: National Center for Employee Ownership.

Zachary, Lois J. 2005. *Creating a Mentoring Culture*. Hoboken: Jossey-Bass.

WorldatWork Courses (www.worldatwork.org/education)

W1: Introduction to Work-Life Effectiveness — Successful Work-Life Programs to Attract, Motivate and Retain Employees Understand the Impact of Work-Life Effectiveness

W2: The Flexible Workplace — Strategies for Your Organization Heighten Employee and Organizational Effectiveness

T1: Total Rewards Management

T4: Strategic Communication in Total Rewards

Additional Resources

Barkdoll, Gerald L. "Individual Personality and Organizational Culture or Let's Change this Place So I Feel More Comfortable." www.pamij.com/barkdoll.html.

Baryon, G. Michael. 2006. "What Happens When the Harassment is Personal." *Journal of Medical Group Practice*, January.

Baryon, G. Michael. 1999. "Personal Harassment Creates Liability." *Healthcare Risk Management*, March.

Baryon, G. Michael. 1989. "The End-of-Story Manager." *Personnel Administrator*.

Blanchard, Ken; Sheldon Bowles. *Gung Ho!*. 1998. New York: William Morrow and Company.

Blanchard, Ken; Jesse Stoner. 2003. *Full Stream Ahead!* San Francisco: Barrett-Koehler.

Bridges, William. 1992. *The Character of Organizations*. Palo Alto: Davies-Black Publishing.

Collins, James C.; Jerry I. Porras. 1994. *Built to Last: Successful Habits of Visionary Companies*. New York: Harper Business.

Denison, Daniel R. 1990. *Corporate Culture and Organizational Effectiveness*. New York: John Wiley & Sons.

Fortune, 2006. "100 Best Companies to Work For." January.

Fortune Magazine, 2005. "Jack Welch: Doing Strategy Right." April.

Fortune Magazine, 2005. "The Wegmans Way." January.

Gibson, James L.; John M. Ivancevich; James H. Donnelly, Jr. 1991. *Organizations*. Homewood: Irwin Publishers.

Harris, Thomas E.; John C. Sherblom. 2005. *Small Group and Team Communication*. Boston: Pearson Education.

Ludwick, Ruth; Mary Cipriano Silva. 2000. "Nursing Around the World: Cultural Values and Ethical Conflicts." *Online Journal of Issues in Nursing*, August.

McShane, Steven L.; Mary Ann Von Gilnow. 2000. *Organizational Behavior*. New York: Irwin/McGraw-Hill Higher Education.

Pearce, John A., III; Richard B. Robinson, Jr. 2005. *Strategic Management: Formulation, Implementation and Control*. New York: Irwin/McGraw-Hill.

Schein, Edgar H. 1999. *The Corporate Culture Survival Guide: Sense and Nonsense About Cultural Change*. San Francisco: Jossey-Bass Publishers.

Schein, Edgar H. 1992. *Organizational Culture and Leadership*. San Francisco: Jossey-Bass Publishers.

Watson Wyatt Worldwide. 2002. *Strategic Rewards — Charting the Course Forward: Maximizing the Value of Reward Programs*. www.watsonwyatt.com

Welch, Jack; Suzy Welch. 2005. *Winning*. New York: HarperCollins Publishers.

Web Site Resources

ANA Nursing World: www.nursingworld.com

Australian Bureau of Statistics: http://www.abs.gov.au/

Container Store: www.containerstore.com

Employment & Workplace Relations Services for Australians: http://www.workplace.gov.au/

High Court of Australia: www.hcourt.gov.au

NIOSH - National institute for Occupational Safety & Health: http://www.cdc.gov/niosh/homepage.html

U.S. Bureau of Labor Statistics: http://www.bls.gov/

Wegmans: www.wegmans.com